From Wounded *To* Wonders

*Overcoming Brokenness and
Walking in God's Restoration*

APOSTLE LUDLOW HAYNES

Wounded To Wonders
Overcoming Brokenness and Walking in God's Restoration

Published by Cornerstone Publishing

A Division of Cornerstone Creativity Group LLC
Info@thecornerstonepublishers.com
www.thecornerstonepublishers.com

Author's Contact

To book the author to speak at your next event or to order bulk copies of this book, please, use the information below:

Phone: 516:849-9625.
Email: Apostlehaynes50@gmail.com

Printed in the United States of America.

DEDICATION

To my wife, Co-Pastor Cecile Haynes, my children,
church members, and people all over the world who
have experienced or know someone who has gone
through a wounded experience.

CONTENTS

DEDICATION iii

WHY THIS BOOK? vii

1. The Hidden Scars Of Trauma 1

2. When Pain Becomes Identity 11

3. From Bitterness To Beauty 21

4. The God Who Sees The Broken 41

5. Breaking Generational Chains 53

6. The Healing Power Of Forgiveness 65

7. The Journey Of Inner Healing 75

8. Restoring Relationships 83

9. Wonders Of Wholeness 101

10. Meeting The God Of Wonders 113

CONCLUSION 127

WHY THIS BOOK?

I didn't set out to write a book merely for the sake of writing. I wrote this because I have lived it, witnessed it, and carried its weight in my own heart.

For as long as I can remember, I have seen the pain hidden within families. I have witnessed mothers—some raped, some abused—bearing silent wounds that overflow into anger, bitterness, and shame. I have seen fathers drown their trauma in alcohol, allowing their brokenness to curse rather than nurture their homes. I have watched children in those homes cry silently at night, unsure why their parents weep or why their family feels so unsafe.

Growing up amidst that pain, I know what it feels like to carry family secrets as a child, to be treated in ways that make you feel rejected and unwanted. As a young person, you cannot comprehend it; you only sense that something is profoundly wrong—that love feels absent and that you must fight for recognition, even if it means acting out to be seen or heard. That kind of woundedness leaves marks on your soul long before anyone else can notice.

However, I am writing this book not just because of my wounds but also because of my healing. I discovered that no matter how deep the hurt or how heavy the shame, God has the power to transform wounds into wonders. I have lived long enough to understand that pain doesn't have to be the final chapter. The bitterness of yesterday can give way to the beauty of tomorrow.

The truth is this: **you may be wounded, but you are not wasted. You may be broken, but you are not beyond repair. You may carry scars, but those scars can become your testimony. You are still a wonder.**

This book is a journey—a path that will lead you from hidden scars and broken identities into the healing embrace of God's restoration. Along the way, I will share not only my story but also the stories of men and women in Scripture who were wounded by life yet transformed by God. From Mephibosheth, who was crippled by a fall yet invited to dine at the king's table, to Rahab, marked by her past but woven into the very lineage of Jesus—these testimonies remind us that woundedness is never the end.

I pray that as you read, you will see yourself in these pages. Perhaps your wounds stem from an absent parent, a betrayal, a loss, or abuse that you dare not speak of. Or maybe your pain is quiet, hidden from the world, yet it whispers to you in the night. No matter your story, know this: God has not forgotten you. He sees you. And He calls you not just by your pain, but by your potential.

This is why I wrote this book—so you can believe again. So you can lift your head and understand that your story does not end with brokenness. So you can walk the same journey I did: from wounded... to wonder.

CHAPTER ONE

THE HIDDEN SCARS OF TRAUMA

Life presents us with two types of wounds: those that are visible and those that remain unseen.

When a child scrapes a knee, we rush to apply bandages. When someone breaks a bone, we place it in a cast until it heals. These visible wounds—though painful—are easily recognized and often treated with time and care.

In contrast, some wounds leave no visible marks on the body. These silent injuries bleed within the soul, manifesting as trauma, rejection, shame, and abuse. Unlike physical wounds, these invisible scars are not treated in hospitals but are carried in the heart for years, sometimes a lifetime.

This book focuses on these hidden scars of trauma.

VISIBLE VS. INVISIBLE WOUNDS

Psychologists tell us that the mind often retains memories of pain far longer than the body. A bruise heals, but the memory of betrayal lingers. A cut closes, yet the sting of rejection resurfaces in unexpected ways. Many who appear "fine" on the outside are quietly fractured on the inside.

Consider Joseph from the Bible. His brothers didn't stab him with a knife, but they wounded him deeply when they stripped him of his robe, threw him into a pit, and sold him into slavery. These wounds were invisible; no one passing by in Egypt could see the scar of betrayal on his heart. Yet those hidden wounds shaped his journey until God restored him.

Similarly, Tamar, the daughter of King David, suffered greatly when her brother Amnon violated her. Scripture notes, "she lived in her brother Absalom's house, desolate" (2 Samuel 13:20). Desolate. She bore an invisible wound that society overlooked, hidden behind closed doors. While her body healed, her soul carried the scar of violation.

In my years of ministry, I have encountered individuals who smiled in public but cried every night in secret.

People who dressed well, worked hard, and appeared successful, yet felt like broken children inside. Their trauma was invisible, but it was as real as any visible wound.

The truth is that invisible wounds can be more dangerous than visible ones because they often go untreated for decades. When we fail to recognize the wound, we do not seek healing.

THE LASTING IMPACT OF CHILDHOOD TRAUMA AND FAMILY SECRETS

Childhood should be a time of innocence, laughter, and trust. Yet for many, it becomes the breeding ground for trauma. The words of a parent, the absence of a father, the violence of abuse, or the silence of neglect shape a child's heart, leaving marks that time alone cannot erase.

Research confirms what many of us instinctively know: childhood trauma has lifelong effects. The renowned **Adverse Childhood Experiences (ACE) Study** shows that children who experience abuse, neglect, or household dysfunction are significantly more likely to struggle with depression, substance abuse, fractured relationships, and even chronic health issues in adulthood. The higher the ACE score, the greater the risk of poor outcomes later in life.

- Children of absent or abusive fathers are twice as likely to battle addiction.

- One in four girls and one in six boys experience sexual abuse before age 18, often resulting in deep emotional scars.

- Adults who faced multiple adverse experiences as children are **four times more likely** to suffer from depression and **twelve times more likely** to attempt suicide.

These statistics represent real stories—neighbors, church members, coworkers, or perhaps ourselves. Trauma rewrites the narrative of a life.

Family secrets inflict additional pain. When children are not told the truth, they fill in the gaps themselves, often blaming themselves and forming harsh conclusions: *"It must be my fault Dad left. I must have done something wrong. Maybe I was never wanted."* Silence becomes a form of abuse. Secrets breed shame, which can imprison both children and adults, preventing them from ever feeling truly free.

I witnessed this firsthand while growing up.

MY OWN WOUNDED BEGINNINGS

I was one of those children.

I grew up in a family where secrets were kept from the children. Things were hidden, left unspoken, and without explanation, I carried confusion in my heart. I felt rejected and unwanted. Because I did not understand the pain my parents were experiencing, I believed their anger was my fault.

When my parents yelled, I thought: *What did I do wrong? Why am I being shouted at? Why don't they love me?*

What I didn't realize then was that my parents were also wounded. They had endured their own trauma, and sometimes, out of their brokenness, they took their frustrations out on us. As a child, I could not see that; I only felt the sting of their anger.

I remember thinking I had to cause trouble to be noticed, to act out to be seen, to create mischief just to be recognized. It wasn't that I wanted to be bad; I was desperate for acknowledgment. I was a child crying for love in the only way I knew how.

But inside, the wound grew. The more I felt rejected, the more I believed I was worthless. That sense of worthlessness is a heavy burden for a child to bear. It shapes self-perception, whispers into teenage years, and follows into adulthood.

Yet this is not where my story ends. God, in His mercy, met me in my woundedness and revealed that what I thought disqualified me was actually the soil where His wonder would grow.

THE ECHO OF TRAUMA IN ADULT LIFE

The wounds of childhood do not simply vanish as we grow taller or graduate. They echo into adult life.

- The child who felt unloved may become the adult who sabotages relationships, perpetually anticipating abandonment.

- The child who was silenced may transform into an adult unable to express emotions, burying pain beneath anger or withdrawal.

- The child who carried family secrets may evolve into an adult who mistrusts everyone, fearing that intimacy will only lead to betrayal. Many of those I have counseled were not responding to their current circumstances; they were reacting to past wounds. A husband yells at his wife, not because of her words, but because he still hears the belittling voice of his father. A woman hides her emotions, not out of coldness, but because she was once told, *"Stop crying or I'll give you something to cry about."*

Unhealed trauma becomes a filter through which we perceive life. We do not see reality as it is; we see it through the lens of our wounds.

BIBLICAL WITNESS TO HIDDEN SCARS

Scripture is not silent about hidden wounds.

- **Mephibosheth** was crippled when a nurse dropped him while fleeing danger. Through no fault of his own, he was left lame, living in shame and fear in a place called *Lo-Debar*, which means "a place of nothing." Though his physical condition was visible, his true wound was invisible—the wound of rejection and fear. Yet King David sought him out and brought him to sit at the king's table (2 Samuel 9).

- **Hagar**, Sarah's servant, was cast into the wilderness with her child. Alone and rejected, she wept. Yet in her lowest moment, God appeared to her, prompting her to declare, *"You are the God who sees me"* (Genesis 16:13).

- **Jesus Himself** bore invisible wounds. Isaiah prophesied, *"He was despised and rejected by men,*

7

a man of sorrows, and acquainted with grief" (Isaiah 53:3). While the nails pierced His body, rejection pierced His heart. He understands the pain of hidden scars.

The Bible does not shy away from trauma. It acknowledges it and presents a God who heals.

MODERN FACES OF TRAUMA

Today, trauma manifests in many forms:

- A child growing up in a home where a parent battles addiction.

- A teenager relentlessly mocked for being different.

- A young girl molested by someone she trusted.

- A boy left wondering why his father never returned.

These wounds may not leave visible bruises, but they deeply impact destinies. If left unhealed, they can lead to broken marriages, substance abuse, depression, and cycles of generational pain.

Statistics reveal that children from fatherless homes are:

- 4 times more likely to live in poverty.

- 7 times more likely to become pregnant as teens,

- More likely to struggle in school, with the law, and with their identity.

Behind each statistic lies a wounded soul.

HOPE FOR THE WOUNDED

However, here lies the wonder: wounds do not define the end of our story.

The same God who saw Hagar in the wilderness, who lifted Mephibosheth from Lo-Debar, and who restored Joseph to a place of influence—He is the God who sees your hidden scars.

Healing begins with recognition. You cannot heal what you will not name. Thus, honesty before God is crucial. When we approach Him and say, *"Lord, this is my wound. This is where it hurts. This is where I feel rejected,"* He begins to pour His healing oil into our wounds.

Psalm 147:3 proclaims, *"He heals the brokenhearted and binds up their wounds."*

Invisible wounds are real, but the healing of God is even more profound.

REFLECTION SUMMARY

- Not all wounds are visible, but all wounds are felt.

- Childhood trauma leaves deep marks that resonate into adulthood.

- Family secrets multiply shame and silence.

- The Bible is filled with individuals bearing hidden scars whom God restored.

- Healing begins when we bring our wounds into the light of God's presence.

A Prayer for Healing

Father, You are the One who sees beyond what others can perceive. You look past our smiles and touch the hidden scars within. Today, I lift up every person reading these words; every man, woman, and child who carries invisible wounds from their past. Heal the places that no one else can reach. Silence the lies of shame and rejection. Remind them that they are not forgotten, not abandoned, and not worthless. Lord, transform their wounds into testimonies and their pain into purpose. Teach them to recognize that they are still Your wonder. In Jesus' name, Amen.

Chapter Two

WHEN PAIN BECOMES IDENTITY

Every person is born with an identity. Long before your first cry, long before your first wound, God spoke destiny over you. He called you His own. He declared that you were created in His image and likeness, chosen, loved, and set apart.

However, for many of us, that identity gets interrupted by pain. Abuse, rejection, abandonment, betrayal — these experiences wound us. Wounds whisper lies about who we are. Over time, if those lies are not confronted, they begin to sound like truth. Pain starts to rename us, and trauma shapes the mirror we look into.

Instead of hearing God's voice say, "You are Mine," we hear pain say, "You are nothing."

HOW PAIN BECOMES IDENTITY

Pain has two sides: the event — the moment something painful happens to you — and the meaning — the story you tell yourself about what that event says about you.

When a father leaves his family, the event is abandonment. The meaning often becomes, "I was not worth staying for." When abuse occurs, the event is violation. The meaning often becomes, "I am dirty. I am damaged goods." When harsh words are spoken — "You'll never amount to anything!" — the event is verbal abuse. The meaning becomes, "I am worthless. I will never succeed."

The human heart is vulnerable, especially in childhood. It cannot always separate what happened to it from who it is. Thus, pain takes root, shaping our deepest identity.

Psychologists call this internalization — the process by which external wounds become internal labels. But as children of God, we know these are not truths; they are lies spoken by pain.

Until those lies are confronted, they act like chains, determining how we live, relate, and see ourselves.

THE STATISTICS BEHIND IDENTITY WOUNDS

Science confirms what Scripture and life experience reveal: trauma does not simply end with the event; it reshapes identity.

The Adverse Childhood Experiences (ACE) study, one of the largest investigations into childhood trauma, found that the more traumatic experiences a child endures, the more likely they are to face depression, addiction, suicide, and relational struggles in adulthood.

- Children who suffer rejection or abandonment are **three times more likely** to face identity issues and low self-esteem as adults.

- Survivors of childhood sexual abuse are **more than twice as likely** to battle shame-based identities, often struggling to see themselves as pure or worthy of love.

- Adults who grew up with family secrets, neglect, or emotional abuse are disproportionately represented in addiction recovery programs — not because they are weak, but because trauma reshaped their self-view.

These numbers are not just data points; they represent people's lives, the quiet struggles behind the faces we see in church pews, workplaces, and our families.

BIBLICAL WITNESS TO IDENTITY WOUNDED BY PAIN

The Bible is filled with men and women whose identities were distorted by trauma. Their stories mirror our own.

- **Naomi**: Once known as "pleasant," her grief after losing her husband and sons was so consuming that she renamed herself Mara, meaning "bitter." Pain tried to rename her.

- **Mephibosheth**: After being dropped as a child, he grew up crippled and living in shame. When brought before King David, he called himself a "dead dog" (2 Samuel 9:8). Though born into royalty, he believed he was worthless.

- **The woman at the well**: Rejected by five husbands and living in shame, she was labeled as immoral by society. She avoided crowds, coming to draw water at noon to escape gossip. Her pain dictated her name.

- **Gideon**: When God called him a "mighty warrior," he argued back: "How can I save Israel?

My clan is the weakest, and I am the least in my family" (Judges 6:15). Pain made him see himself as small when God saw him as mighty.

Each of these individuals illustrates a truth: pain has the power to rename, but God always calls us back to who we truly are.

MY OWN STORY OF PAIN AND IDENTITY

I cannot write about this without sharing my own journey.

As a child, I grew up in an environment where anger and family secrets were normal. There were unspoken truths, unanswered questions, and the silence itself was a wound.

When my parents yelled, I didn't understand why. I didn't know the struggles they had endured. All I felt was the sting of rejection. In my young heart, I concluded: "It must be me. I am the problem. I am unwanted."

That lie attached itself to me like a shadow, following me into school, friendships, and every corner of my self-image. I believed I had to cause trouble to be seen. I believed love had to be earned through performance. I believed I was not good enough.

Looking back, I see how pain tried to rewrite my identity. But God, in His mercy, spoke louder. He whispered truth into the lies, and slowly I began to realize that my wound was not my name.

THE CONSEQUENCES OF LIVING FROM A WOUNDED IDENTITY

When identity is shaped by pain instead of God's truth, the consequences ripple across every area of life.

- **Broken Relationships** – A person who sees themselves as unworthy may sabotage love, expecting abandonment and pushing people away before they can be hurt again.

- **Addiction and Self-Destruction** – Those who feel "dirty" or "worthless" may numb themselves with alcohol, drugs, or destructive habits. Pain seeks escape when not healed.

- **Fear of God's Love** – If a parent wounded you, it becomes easy to project that image onto God. Instead of seeing Him as a loving Father, you expect rejection.

- **Generational Cycles** – Wounded identities often lead to wounded parenting. Those who were rejected may repeat patterns without realizing it.

Research supports this. Adults with histories of

childhood rejection are twice as likely to face divorce, three times more likely to struggle with depression, and more likely to perpetuate cycles of rejection with their own children.

Pain does not just wound an individual; it attempts to wound a lineage.

JESUS RESTORES IDENTITY

Into this brokenness steps Jesus. His mission was not only to save us from sin but to heal the brokenhearted and restore identity.

- To Naomi, He gave Ruth, and through her lineage came David and ultimately Jesus — turning "bitter" back into "pleasant."

- To Mephibosheth, He sent King David, who lifted him from Lo-Debar to the king's table — a prophetic picture of how Christ restores us to sonship.

- To the woman at the well, He offered living water, making her a voice that brought her whole village to salvation.

- To Gideon, He affirmed, "Go in the strength you have... am I not sending you?" (Judges 6:14). God renamed him according to his calling, not his fear.

17

And to us, He says: "You are my beloved child. You are chosen. You are redeemed. You are more than a conqueror."

PRACTICAL STEPS TO RESTORE IDENTITY

1. Name the Wound

Healing begins with honesty. Pretending you are not hurt keeps you bound. Say it aloud: "I was abandoned. I was abused. I was rejected." Bringing the wound into the light is the first step to healing.

2. Separate Event from Identity

What happened to you is not who you are. Abuse is something you suffered — it is not your name. Rejection was an action done to you — it does not define your worth.

3. Replace Lies With Truth

Speak Scripture over yourself:

- "I am fearfully and wonderfully made" (Psalm 139:14).

- "I am chosen, holy, and dearly loved" (Colossians 3:12).

- "I am more than a conqueror through Christ" (Romans 8:37).

4. Forgive and Release

Unforgiveness keeps you tied to the one who hurt you. Forgiveness does not excuse sin; it breaks the chain. It is saying, "You will not define me anymore."

5. Seek Safe Community

Healing happens in connection. Surround yourself with people who call you by your true name — beloved, valued, chosen — not the labels of your wound.

6. Renew the Mind Daily

Romans 12:2 says we are transformed by renewing our minds. Healing is not a one-time event but a daily process of replacing lies with truth.

MY TURNING POINT

My healing came when I allowed God to confront my false identity. For years, I believed I was unwanted. But as I grew in Christ, I heard a new voice: "You are my beloved son. You are chosen. You are mine."

It did not happen overnight, but with each truth I embraced, a lie fell away. The shadow of rejection gave way to the light of sonship.

That same God who restored me is able to restore you.

REFLECTION SUMMARY

- Pain tries to rename you, but God has already named you.

- Trauma whispers lies that can feel like truth if left unchallenged.

- Living from a wounded identity distorts relationships, faith, and generations.

- Jesus restores identity, lifting us from woundedness into wonder.

- Healing begins with honesty, forgiveness, truth, and daily renewal.

Prayer for Restored Identity

Father, I come before You with the wounds of my heart. For too long, pain has told me who I am. Trauma has whispered lies I believed. But today, I reject those lies and choose to embrace Your truth. I am not what happened to me — I am who You say I am. I am chosen, beloved, and redeemed. Heal my heart. Renew my mind. Break every chain of false identity. Restore me to the fullness of who You created me to be. In Jesus' name, Amen.

CHAPTER THREE

FROM BITTERNESS TO BEAUTY

B itterness is one of the heaviest burdens a human soul can bear. It often remains quiet and hidden in the corners of the heart, gradually eroding the spirit. Unlike grief, which follows a natural course—intense at first and then softening over time—bitterness does not ease or fade. Instead, it calcifies and hardens, transforming sorrow into a sharp edge and disappointment into poison.

Bitterness traps the heart in a prison of resentment, erecting walls around our emotions so high that even joy cannot penetrate. It distorts our perception, casting a shadow over everything we see. A conversation with a friend becomes an opportunity to feel misunderstood, a kind gesture is met with suspicion, and a blessing feels inadequate. To the bitter soul, life is never enough, and others become targets for the pain they harbor within.

While we often think of bitterness as mere anger toward others, it is much more complex at its core. Bitterness is essentially *unprocessed* pain—grief that was never allowed to heal, disappointment that was never released, betrayal that was never forgiven, and heartbreak that was never surrendered to God.

When left unaddressed, pain festers like an untreated wound. What could have healed with time and care becomes infected, spreading its poison throughout every aspect of life. That is the essence of bitterness.

Bitterness whispers cruel lies into the soul:

- *"Life cheated me."*

- *"God failed me."*

- *"People cannot be trusted."*

- *"I will never be whole again."*

These whispers feel true, reinforced by pain and echoed by experiences. Soon, we no longer see bitterness as something we *carry*; we begin to perceive it as something we *are*.

Yet, here lies the hope: bitterness is not the conclusion of our story. It is not a life sentence. Even in the toughest soil, God can cultivate beauty. Even in the most bitter circumstances, He can bring forth sweetness. He is the One who transforms ashes into beauty, turns mourning into dancing, and converts the soil of bitterness into a garden of grace.

THE BITTER WATERS OF MARAH

In the book of Exodus, there is a poignant image that illustrates a deep truth. After the Israelites crossed the Red Sea, they journeyed for three days in the desert without finding water. Imagine their thirst, exhaustion, and desperation. Finally, they arrived at a place called Marah, and their hearts filled with relief at the sight of water shimmering in the desert sun. However, when they tried to drink, they discovered the water was bitter—undrinkable, disappointing, and almost mocking in its promise of refreshment.

This moment encapsulates the essence of bitterness: when life appears to offer hope but instead delivers disappointment. What you expected to bring joy leaves you feeling empty.

The people grumbled, expressing their anger towards Moses and God. In response, God showed Moses a piece of wood and instructed him to throw it into the water. Miraculously, the waters became sweet (Exodus 15:22–25).

This piece of wood foreshadowed the cross of Christ. Just as the wood transformed bitter water into sweetness, the cross has the power to turn our bitter experiences into sources of healing. While bitterness may be a reality, it can be redeemed when touched by the cross.

This story is not merely historical; it serves as a living metaphor. Each of us has our own "Marah," a place of bitter waters: a failed marriage, betrayal, loss, or an unfulfilled dream. Yet, just as God intervened for Israel, He can intervene for us. He does not leave us to endure bitterness indefinitely; He has a way of transforming it into sweetness.

Even before we delve into Naomi's story, we recognize this truth: God specializes in meeting His people at the waters of Marah. He does not ignore our bitterness; He transforms it. He does not condemn us for tasting bitterness; He redeems it.

NAOMI'S STORY: WHEN LIFE TURNS BITTER

Few biblical figures illustrate this truth more vividly than Naomi. She began her story with promise. Married to Elimelech, she lived in Bethlehem, literally known as "the house of bread." However, when famine struck, her family left Bethlehem for Moab, a foreign land. What seemed like a temporary solution turned into years of heartache.

In Moab, Naomi's husband died. Her two sons married Moabite women, but tragically, both sons also died. Naomi was left with two widowed daughters-in-law and a heart filled with grief.

When she finally returned to Bethlehem, the women of the city recognized her and exclaimed, *"Can this be Naomi?"* Her response was striking:

"Don't call me Naomi," she told them. "Call me Mara, for the Almighty has made my life very bitter. I went away full, but the Lord has brought me back empty" (Ruth 1:20–21).

The name Naomi means "pleasant," while Mara means "bitter." Pain had redefined her. Trauma had renamed her.

How many of us have experienced this? When life hits so hard that you feel like a different person. You wake up one day and think, *"I used to be joyful, hopeful, pleasant — now I am just bitter."*

THE PSYCHOLOGY OF BITTERNESS

Modern psychology aligns with Scripture: bitterness is destructive. Studies show that chronic bitterness can lead to depression, anxiety, high blood pressure, and even a weakened immune system. Psychologist Carsten Wrosch describes bitterness as "the unhealthiest emotion" because, unlike anger or grief, it lingers instead of fading.

Unresolved grief turns into bitterness when:

- We cannot make sense of loss.

- We believe life is unfair and remain stuck in "why me?"

- We harbor resentment against God, others, or even ourselves.

The Bible warns us: *"See to it that no bitter root grows up to cause trouble and defile many"* (Hebrews 12:15). Like roots, bitterness initially grows unseen but eventually spreads, choking out joy and contaminating relationships.

NAOMI'S TURNING POINT

Though Naomi renamed herself Mara, God had not forgotten her. Beside her stood Ruth, her Moabite daughter-in-law, who declared, *"Where you go I will go, and where you stay I will stay. Your people will be my people and your God my God"* (Ruth 1:16).

Ruth became God's instrument of restoration in Naomi's life. Through Ruth's marriage to Boaz, Naomi's family line was redeemed. In time, Ruth bore a son, Obed, and the women of the town said to Naomi: *"Praise be to the Lord, who this day has not left you without a guardian-redeemer... He will renew your life and sustain you in your old age"* (Ruth 4:14–15).

The same woman who once declared, *"The Lord has brought me back empty,"* now held a child in her arms — a symbol of fullness, restoration, and legacy.

Naomi's story serves as a powerful reminder: even when bitterness tries to redefine us, God continues to craft chapters of beauty.

THE COST OF BITTERNESS

Before we explore the theme of beauty, we must confront the true cost of bitterness. Underestimating its dangers only strengthens its grip. Scripture refers to bitterness as a "root" because it burrows deep beneath the surface, initially hidden, but eventually emerging and permeating every aspect of our lives (Hebrews 12:15). Let's examine how bitterness affects the human soul.

1. Bitterness Isolates Us

When Naomi returned to her hometown of Bethlehem, the women rushed to greet her with joy, exclaiming, "Naomi is back!" However, Naomi was unable to hear their welcome; she was consumed by her pain. Instead of embracing their affection, she rebuffed it, saying, *"Don't call me Naomi. Call me Mara, for the Lord has made my life very bitter."*

This illustrates the first cost of bitterness: it isolates us. It blinds us to those who care. A bitter heart struggles to accept love because it feels alien when one has become accustomed to loss.

In modern life, this manifests as someone who avoids social gatherings, finding it unbearable to witness others' joy. It may also look like rejecting encouragement, as bitterness whispers, *"They don't really mean it. You are alone."*

Isolation is perilous because healing often occurs through connection. Bitterness persuades us to withdraw from the very community that God has provided to support us.

2. Bitterness Distorts Our View of God

Naomi did not merely blame her circumstances; she shifted the blame onto God. She lamented, *"The Almighty has dealt very bitterly with me. I went away full, but the Lord has brought me back empty"* (Ruth 1:20–21).

In her eyes, God was not her ally but her adversary. Her bitterness painted Him as harsh, cruel, and punishing. Yet, unbeknownst to her, God was already orchestrating a plan for redemption through Ruth and Boaz.

This is the insidious nature of bitterness: it distorts our understanding of God. Instead of viewing Him as a loving Father, we see Him as a cold judge. Rather than trusting in His providence, we question His motives. Our pain becomes the lens through which we interpret His character.

This distortion prevents many believers from experiencing intimacy with God. They may attend church, yet their worship remains guarded. They pray, but their words feel hollow because in their hearts, they question, *"Why didn't You stop it? Why did You allow it?"*

Bitterness creates distance, not because God withdraws, but because our perception of Him becomes clouded.

3. Bitterness Poisons Relationships

Bitterness seldom stays confined within a single heart. Like a toxin, it seeps into relationships. Bitter individuals often push away those who try to help. Even genuine acts of love can feel overwhelming to accept, as bitterness filters every interaction through suspicion and cynicism.

A friend offering encouragement may be met with sarcasm. A spouse trying to comfort might encounter coldness. A child expressing affection could be dismissed. Unbeknownst to them, bitterness erects walls around the heart, making intimacy impossible.

This is why Proverbs warns, *"A bitter heart knows its own sorrows"* (Proverbs 14:10). Bitterness becomes self-consuming. Just as Naomi's bitterness initially blinded her to Ruth's loyalty, it blinds us to the love right beside us.

If left unchecked, bitterness can harm marriages, divide families, and fracture friendships. Its poison affects not only the bitter person but also those closest to them.

4. Bitterness Keeps Us Stuck

Perhaps the greatest cost of bitterness is that it keeps us anchored to the past. Naomi struggled to move beyond her losses — her husband, her sons, her stability. Though she stood in Bethlehem, the "house of bread," bitterness convinced her she was still empty.

This is the cruel trap of bitterness: it ties us to yesterday. We replay betrayals repeatedly, reliving disappointments like a movie on a loop. We rehearse our losses until they become our identity.

As long as we hold onto bitterness, we cannot move forward. We remain blind to new possibilities and unable to embrace new joy. We stay trapped in what was, unable to step into what could be.

Modern counselors refer to this as "rumination" — the cycle of replaying painful events without resolution. It keeps people emotionally frozen, preventing them from processing grief in a healthy way. Spiritually, it hinders us from experiencing the abundant life Jesus promised.

Many of us understand the feeling of being trapped in bitterness. It's akin to drinking poison while expecting someone else to suffer. In reality, it harms us far more than it affects those we resent.

FROM BITTERNESS TO BEAUTY: GOD'S PROCESS

Naomi's story illustrates that although bitterness has its costs, it does not signify the end of our journey. God specializes in transforming bitter seasons into fertile ground for beauty. However, this transformation is gradual; healing unfolds step by step as we invite God to touch the hardened areas of our hearts.

Here are four ways God guides us from bitterness to beauty:

1. Honest Lament Before God

Naomi expressed her feelings candidly. She did not pretend to be fine but stood in her community and proclaimed, *"The Almighty has made my life very bitter"* (Ruth 1:20). Despite her pain clouding her theology, her honesty opened the door for God to meet her.

This is the initial step in the process — lament. Scripture is rich with examples of lament. The book of Psalms, often referred to as Israel's prayer book, includes not only songs of praise but also cries of despair:

- *"How long, Lord? Will you forget me forever?"* (Psalm 13:1).

- *"Why, my soul, are you downcast? Why so disturbed within me?"* (Psalm 42:5).

- *"My God, my God, why have you forsaken me?"* (Psalm 22:1).

Even Jesus, while on the cross, expressed lament. Lament is not a sign of unbelief; rather, it is an act of faith that brings our pain to God instead of concealing it.

2. The Gift of Loyal Love

Although Naomi felt abandoned, she was not alone. Ruth remained by her side, steadfast in her commitment: *"Where you go, I will go... your God will be my God"* (Ruth 1:16). Ruth's loyalty was a manifestation of God's provision. Even in Naomi's bitterness, God sent someone to represent His unwavering love.

God often places "Ruths" in our lives — individuals who remain when others depart, reminding us of hope when we cannot see it ourselves. Sometimes these are faithful friends, counselors, spouses, mentors, or church communities.

Though Naomi may have felt empty, she was not forsaken. Ruth's presence was evidence that God's love had not abandoned her.

3. Redemption Through God's Providence

Naomi could not have scripted her redemption. She couldn't arrange Ruth's encounter with Boaz or orchestrate the events that led to her family line being restored. God was at work behind the scenes, even when Naomi felt abandoned by Him.

This illustrates how providence functions. God takes ordinary events—such as a woman gleaning in a field and a man showing kindness—and weaves them into extraordinary redemption. In hindsight, Naomi could see that God had been active all along.

Providence reassures us that God is never absent in our moments of bitterness. His hand may be hidden, but it is always at work.

4. Embracing the New Chapter

When Ruth gave birth to Obed, the women of Bethlehem placed the child in Naomi's arms and said, *"Praise be to the Lord, who this day has not left you without a guardian-redeemer"* (Ruth 4:14). Naomi, once "empty," was now full.

However, Naomi had to embrace this new chapter. She needed to open her arms to Obed and allow herself to feel joy again. This is often the hardest step—granting ourselves permission to live beyond our bitterness.

Some people remain in Mara even when Bethlehem is within reach. They cling to their bitterness because it feels safer than risking hope. Yet God calls us to let go of the old name and embrace the new.

PRACTICAL STEPS TO MOVE FROM BITTERNESS TO BEAUTY

While God ultimately transforms our bitterness into beauty, we must actively cooperate with His process. Healing often requires intentional choices—small but powerful steps that loosen the grip of bitterness and open our hearts to new life. Here are some practical ways to begin that journey:

1. Name the Bitterness

Healing begins with recognition. You cannot heal what you do not name. Bitterness thrives in vagueness—in the unspoken, unacknowledged corners of the heart. However, once you identify it, its power begins to diminish.

Ask yourself honestly: *Who am I bitter toward?* Is it God, for not preventing what happened? Is it a parent, for their absence or abuse? Is it a friend, for betrayal? Or is it yourself, for mistakes you cannot seem to forgive?

Naomi's healing began when she expressed, *"The Almighty has made my life very bitter"* (Ruth 1:20). Acknowledging her bitterness marked not the conclusion of her journey, but the start of her liberation.

2. Release Forgiveness

Forgiveness is one of the most challenging yet freeing steps in the healing process. It does not mean excusing the wrong, downplaying the pain, or pretending it never happened. Instead, forgiveness is about releasing the debt — choosing to let go of the poison of resentment that burdens your soul.

Bitterness insists, *"They owe me, and until they pay, I will not heal."* In contrast, forgiveness proclaims, *"I release them, and I will no longer allow their actions to define my life."*

Ephesians 4:31–32 urges us: *"Get rid of all bitterness, rage, and anger... Be kind and compassionate to one another, forgiving each other, just as in Christ God forgave you."* Notice the sequence: bitterness departs when forgiveness arrives.

Forgiveness is not merely a one-time emotion; it often requires repeated choices. However, with each act of release, the chains of bitterness loosen.

3. Practice Gratitude

Bitterness thrives on loss, obsessing over what we no longer possess: the relationship, the opportunity, the dream, the child, the health. Gratitude shifts our focus. It does not ignore the loss but reminds us that God has not left us empty-handed.

When Naomi returned to Bethlehem, she lamented, *"I went away full, but the Lord has brought me back empty"* (Ruth 1:21). She couldn't yet recognize that Ruth stood beside her — one of the greatest gifts in her narrative. It was gratitude that would later open her eyes to Ruth's presence and the blessing of Obed.

Gratitude softens the hardened soil of bitterness. Begin with small acts: thank God for a new day, for breath in your lungs, for a loyal friend, for His presence. Like drops of water on parched ground, gratitude gradually revives the heart.

4. Invite God's Perspective

Bitterness deceives us into believing we see the entire picture, convincing us, *"This is all there is. My story is over. My life is ruined."* Yet, God sees from a higher perspective. Where we perceive emptiness, He sees potential. Where we identify endings, He discerns beginnings.

Naomi felt she had lost everything. Yet, from Ruth's womb would come Obed, the grandfather of King David and an ancestor of Jesus Christ. What Naomi viewed as an empty conclusion, God recognized as the foundation for a redemptive history.

Isaiah 55:8–9 reminds us: *"For my thoughts are not your thoughts, neither are your ways my ways… As the heavens are higher than the earth, so are my ways higher than your ways and my thoughts than your thoughts."*

Inviting God's perspective does not mean we will understand everything. Instead, it signifies our trust that His view is broader, deeper, and kinder than our own.

5. Serve Others

Bitterness turns our focus inward, causing life to revolve around our pain, loss, and grievances. One of the quickest ways to break free from bitterness is to serve others. Serving shifts our attention outward, reminding us that we still have something to give.

Jesus exemplified this on the night before His crucifixion. Aware of the betrayal and suffering that awaited Him, He knelt down and washed His disciples' feet (John 13:1–17), choosing service over self-absorption.

When we serve, joy often returns unexpectedly. The smile of someone we've helped, the gratitude of someone we've blessed, and the relief of someone we've comforted become fresh streams in what once felt like a desert. Service does not erase our pain but redeems it by transforming it into purpose.

These steps are not formulas but pathways that create space for God's Spirit to do what only He can — transform bitterness into beauty.

REFLECTION SUMMARY

- Bitterness is unprocessed pain that poisons life.

- Naomi's story illustrates how trauma can rename us, but God can restore.

- Healing involves lament, loyal love, God's providence, and embracing new joy.

- Modern testimonies confirm that bitterness can become beauty.

- Practical steps: naming, forgiving, expressing gratitude, gaining perspective, and serving, guide us toward freedom.

Prayer for Healing from Bitterness

Father, I bring You the bitter places in my life; the losses, betrayals, and disappointments. I confess that bitterness has sometimes hardened my heart. Today, I choose to release it. I choose forgiveness. I choose gratitude. I invite You to touch my bitterness with the cross of Christ and make it sweet again. Restore my joy, renew my hope, and turn my mourning into dancing. Let my story, like Naomi's, move from bitterness to beauty. In Jesus' name, Amen.

CHAPTER FOUR

THE GOD WHO SEES
THE BROKEN

O ne of the deepest longings of the human heart
is to be seen. From childhood to adulthood, we
crave more than just a fleeting glance — we yearn for
recognition, for someone to look into our lives and
affirm, *"I notice you. You matter. I see your pain. I value your
story."* To be seen is to feel that our existence holds
significance, that our tears are not in vain, and that our
journey is not overlooked.

When we are truly seen, our dignity is restored. A smile
from a parent, a word of encouragement from a friend,
or even the kind gaze of a stranger can uplift our spirits.
However, when we are not seen, a different narrative
unfolds.

Brokenness convinces us that we are invisible. Trauma whispers that our suffering is insignificant, that our cries echo into an empty void. Rejection leads us to believe we are forgettable, easily replaced, and discarded without a second thought. Shame creeps in and mocks us, insisting that our past is too messy, too dirty, too shameful for anyone — even God — to care about. Gradually, we begin to live as though we are hidden. We shrink back, cover up, and pretend.

Many who bear wounds grapple with this haunting question: *"Does anyone really see me? Does anyone care enough to look beyond the surface?"* When unanswered, this question can become a profound ache — a loneliness that no amount of busyness or achievement can alleviate.

Yet, woven like a golden thread through the pages of Scripture is this breathtaking truth: God sees. He notices what others overlook and pays attention to what others ignore. He does not turn away when we are hurting. He does not pass by when we are crushed. He does not dismiss what the world devalues.

He is El Roi — *the God who sees the broken.* He sees you not as invisible, but as irreplaceable. He sees you not as discarded, but as destined. He recognizes not only the wounds you carry but also the wonder He instilled within you. His gaze is not casual; it is compassionate. Not distant, but deeply engaged.

This is the God who saw Hagar in the wilderness, Rahab in her shame, and the forgotten ones in the Gospels. And this is the God who sees you, right here, right now.

HAGAR: THE WOMAN WHO NAMED GOD

Hagar's story unfolds in the shadows of another's household. As an Egyptian servant in Sarah's home, she held no power, no voice, and had little control over her own destiny. When Sarah struggled to conceive, she offered Hagar to Abraham—not out of affection for her, but out of desperation for her own legacy.

Hagar complied and bore Abraham's child. Yet, instead of gratitude, she faced Sarah's jealousy and cruelty. The home that should have provided refuge became intolerable, prompting her to flee—pregnant, alone, and unwanted—into the desert wilderness.

In her lowest moment, the angel of the Lord found her by a spring. He didn't just appear in glory and give instructions; He called her by name: *"Hagar, servant of Sarah, where have you come from and where are you going?"* (Genesis 16:8). Being named in the wilderness served as a reminder that her identity was not erased by her suffering.

In awe, Hagar proclaimed: *"You are the God who sees me"* (Genesis 16:13). She bestowed upon God the name El

Roi, meaning the God who sees. An abused servant, she became the first person in Scripture to personally name God. Her brokenness became the very stage on which God revealed Himself.

This is the God we serve: the One who seeks us at our desert springs, who sees us when others cast us aside, and who calls us by name when we feel nameless.

RAHAB: THE GOD WHO SAW BEYOND HER LABEL

In the fortified city of Jericho, Rahab was defined by a single word: prostitute. Her community saw her not as a person but as her occupation. She was tolerated yet despised, used but not respected. To many, her name was synonymous with shame.

However, when the Israelite spies entered Jericho, it was Rahab who welcomed them. Her actions were not merely acts of survival; they were acts of faith. She told the spies, *"I know that the Lord has given you this land… the Lord your God is God in heaven above and on the earth below"* (Joshua 2:9–11).

That confession marked a turning point. While others focused solely on her sin, God recognized her faith. Where others saw a woman ensnared by shame, God saw a woman ready for redemption. When Jericho's walls fell, Rahab and her household were not only spared but welcomed into Israel. She married, had children, and became the great-great-grandmother of King David and an ancestor of Jesus Christ.

Rahab's story teaches us that God's perspective is redemptive. He doesn't merely see our past; He envisions our future. He doesn't dwell on our failures; He recognizes the faith within us, even when it lies buried beneath the rubble of our lives. He looks at the prostitute and sees a matriarch; at the broken, He sees a builder of destiny.

THE BROKEN JESUS SAW

When Jesus walked the earth, His gaze was uniquely profound. He didn't just glance at people; He pierced their hearts with love. His ministry was filled with instances where He noticed the broken that others overlooked.

He saw the **blind beggar** on the roadside in Jericho, crying out, *"Son of David, have mercy on me!"* The crowd tried to silence him, viewing beggars as an inconvenience. But Jesus stopped, called him forward, and restored his sight (Mark 10:46–52). To be seen by Jesus meant having dignity restored.

He saw the **paralyzed man** lowered through the roof by his friends. Before healing his legs, He said, *"Son, your sins are forgiven"* (Mark 2:5). Jesus looked beyond physical brokenness; He recognized the soul's need for healing.

He saw the **widow of Nain** following her son's coffin to burial. While the crowd mourned, Jesus locked eyes with her. Scripture tells us He was "moved with compassion" (Luke 7:13). He halted the funeral procession, touched the coffin, and brought her son back to life. In acknowledging her grief, He restored her future.

He saw the **woman bent over for eighteen years**, crippled and shamed, perhaps unnoticed in the synagogue. Jesus called her forward and said, *"Woman, you are set free"* (Luke 13:12). For nearly two decades, no one truly saw her. But Jesus did.

To be seen by Jesus is to be valued, dignified, and healed. His gaze penetrated shame, uplifted the weary, and restored hope.

THE POWER OF BEING SEEN

Human beings are created for connection. Psychologists emphasize that validation—the feeling of being recognized—is crucial for emotional health. Babies thrive when their parents respond to their cries, spouses flourish when they feel understood, and patients heal more quickly when doctors listen with compassion.

When we are not acknowledged, we suffer. Trauma often leaves behind a hidden wound: *"No one noticed. No one believed me. No one cared."* The experience of being unseen is painful in its own right.

However, everything changes when God sees us. Hagar realized she was not invisible. Rahab discovered she was not disqualified. The broken individuals in the Gospels found that they were not forgotten. God's sight does more than acknowledge; it restores. To be seen by Him is to have our dignity renewed.

GOD SEES YOU IN YOUR BROKENNESS

This truth extends beyond biblical stories; it applies to you right now. In your valley, your desert, your Jericho, and your grief—God sees you.

The psalmist wrote: *"You keep track of all my sorrows. You have collected all my tears in your bottle. You have recorded each one in your book"* (Psalm 56:8). Imagine that—not a single tear goes unnoticed. Not one sleepless night is ignored. Not one prayer goes unheard.

You may feel invisible to others, but you are never invisible to God. He sees not only your wounds but also

47

your worth. He recognizes not only what has broken you but also what He can create through you. He views you not as discarded but as destined.

PRACTICAL STEPS TO LIVE AS ONE WHO IS SEEN

Knowing that God sees us is not just comforting; it is transformative. It is more than a warm notion—it reshapes how we live, how we perceive ourselves, and how we treat others. When you begin to live as someone who is seen by God, your demeanor changes. You no longer walk in shame but in dignity. You no longer feel overlooked but chosen.

Here are four ways this truth can reshape us:

1. Bring Your Brokenness into His Presence

Like Hagar, we must stop running and allow God to meet us at our desert springs. Too often, we hide our wounds, believing they are too messy for Him. We polish our prayers, wear masks of strength, and pretend before others—and even before God Himself. But God cannot heal what remains hidden.

Hagar encountered Him not in a palace or a moment of strength, but in the wilderness, weary, rejected, and afraid. It was there that He revealed Himself as *the God who sees.*

When we dare to bring our brokenness into His presence honestly, we experience the wonder of His gaze. He does not turn away or flinch. He meets us in the rawness of our reality and begins to heal.

2. Receive His New Identity

Rahab had been labeled as a prostitute her entire life. But when God recognized her faith, He rewrote her story. She was no longer defined by her shame but by her role in His redemptive plan.

We, too, must stop wearing the labels of our past. Pain attempts to rename us—*failure, rejected, unworthy, dirty.* Yet when God sees us, He speaks destiny over us—*beloved, chosen, redeemed, called.*

Living as one who is seen means exchanging false names for our true identity. It requires believing that we are not what happened to us, nor what was said about us, nor the worst thing we ever did. We are who God says we are.

3. Pay Attention to His Gaze

In the Gospels, those who encountered Jesus often found something life-changing in His eyes. When He saw the paralytic, He spoke forgiveness. When He saw the widow, He was moved with compassion. When He saw Zacchaeus in the tree, He called him by name. His gaze was never one of condemnation but of restoration.

As we live as people who are seen, we learn to pay attention to His gaze. We begin to view ourselves not through the lens of shame but through the eyes of Christ. His eyes are filled with compassion, mercy, and love.

This transforms everything. Instead of asking, *"How do others see me?"* or *"How do I see myself?"* we ask, *"How does Jesus see me?"* And His gaze empowers us to rise from the ashes of brokenness.

4. See Others Through His Eyes

Finally, living as one who is seen empowers us to extend that same grace to others. When we are dignified by God's gaze, we can dignify the broken around us. We no longer avoid the overlooked; instead, we seek them out. We no longer shun the rejected; we sit with them. We no longer dismiss the broken; we honor them with compassion.

This is how the Kingdom of God spreads: one person seen, who then sees another. One person restored, who then restores another. The God who saw us in our brokenness now invites us to be His eyes in the world.

A STORY OF BEING SEEN

I once met a young man named Daniel who grew up in a home marked by neglect and abuse. For years, he felt invisible—his father barely acknowledged him, his mother was too overwhelmed to listen, and teachers overlooked his quiet pain. As he grew older, rejection shaped his identity, and he carried the labels of *unwanted, forgotten, and worthless.*

But one night, sitting in the back of a small church service, Daniel felt something he had never experienced before: the gaze of God. The preacher spoke from Psalm 34:18, *"The Lord is close to the brokenhearted and saves those who are crushed in spirit."* Daniel wept. In that moment, he realized, *God sees me. God has always seen me.*

That encounter became a turning point. He began to bring his brokenness honestly before God instead of hiding it. He started to embrace a new identity as beloved rather than rejected. As he grew in faith, he learned to see himself through the compassionate eyes of Jesus rather than the condemning eyes of his past. Eventually, Daniel began serving at a youth shelter, where he now tells other broken young men and women, *"You are not invisible. God sees you, just like He saw me."*

Daniel's journey encapsulates the power of bringing brokenness into God's presence, receiving His new identity, paying attention to His gaze, and then extending that same loving sight to others.

REFLECTION SUMMARY

- Brokenness makes us feel invisible, but God sees us fully.

- Hagar discovered Him as *El Roi— the God who sees me.*

- Rahab's label did not limit God's redemption.

- Jesus consistently noticed the people society ignored.

- Living as someone who is seen transforms our identity and relationships.

Prayer to the God Who Sees

El Roi, the God who sees me, I bring You my brokenness. I offer You the places where I feel invisible, forgotten, and overlooked. Thank You for not passing me by. Thank You for seeing me fully — not just my failures, but my potential; not just my wounds, but my worth. Lord, let Your gaze heal me. Restore my dignity. Remind me that I matter to You. Teach me to see others with the same eyes of compassion. In Jesus' name, Amen.

Chapter Five

BREAKING GENERATIONAL CHAINS

Some of the deepest wounds we carry are not solely our own; they are inherited. They echo yesterday's pain, reverberating into today. Generational chains are patterns of brokenness passed from one generation to the next, like an invisible thread woven through family stories. At times, these chains are obvious, while at other times they quietly shape us in ways we scarcely comprehend.

A child grows up with an angry father, vowing never to become like him — only to erupt with the same rage in his own home years later. A daughter raised in neglect, who longed for tenderness, becomes a mother who struggles to show affection, repeating what she experienced. A grandson finds himself drawn to the same addictions that once destroyed his grandfather. Poverty, abuse, and shame often travel through bloodlines like unwelcome guests, knocking on the door of each new generation.

These chains can feel like destiny. You may have thought or said, *"It runs in my family. That's just how we are."* Yet behind that resignation lies the heavy burden of intergenerational pain.

Psychologists refer to this as *intergenerational trauma* — wounds not healed in one generation are passed to the next. Children carry the stress, fears, and dysfunction of their parents, often without awareness. Scripture describes it in ancient terms: "the sins of the fathers" visiting the children to the third and fourth generation (Exodus 20:5). Different words, same reality: brokenness repeats itself unless someone stands up and declares, *"It stops here."*

But here is the hope: those chains, no matter how strong, are not permanent. They may run through your family line, but they do not have to dictate your future. God has the power to break generational chains. What began as a curse can end with you. What has harmed your family does not have to define you. The cross of

Christ proclaims a new reality: you are not bound to repeat what was handed down; instead, you can pass on freedom, healing, and blessing.

UNDERSTANDING GENERATIONAL CHAINS

Generational chains are often invisible at first. They manifest not only in dramatic patterns of addiction or abuse but also in subtle behaviors and mindsets. You may wonder why you react with intense anger to minor triggers, why relationships feel so fragile, or why fear seems to shadow you even when life is stable.

Sometimes, these chains are learned behaviors. Children imitate what they observe. If they witness rage, they learn to express rage. If they observe silence, they learn to remain silent. Other times, they stem from unhealed trauma. A parent who lacks affirmation may struggle to affirm their own children. An abandoned mother may unintentionally pass down insecurity.

Scripture provides vivid examples: Abraham lied out of fear, claiming Sarah was his sister. Later, Isaac repeated the same deceit about Rebekah. Jacob, Isaac's son, became known for his cunning, tricking both his father and brother. Jacob's sons continued the cycle by lying about Joseph's death. A thread of deception ran through generations until God intervened and used Joseph to break the pattern.

This is how chains operate—silent, subtle, yet strong. They can feel like destiny. But God's truth assures us: *chains are not destiny. They can be broken.*

BIBLICAL STORIES OF BROKEN CHAINS

Joseph

Joseph grew up in a dysfunctional family marked by jealousy, favoritism, and betrayal. His brothers sold him into slavery, a wound deep enough to embitter anyone. Yet, when the tables turned and Joseph held power over them in Egypt, he chose not to repay evil with evil. Instead, he declared: *"You meant evil against me, but God meant it for good"* (Genesis 50:20).

Joseph's choice to forgive broke the generational chain of vengeance. What began as betrayal ended as blessing. His decision not only healed him; it preserved a nation.

Gideon

Gideon grew up in a family and community deeply entrenched in idolatry. His father had constructed an altar to Baal, to which everyone bowed. However, when God called Gideon, his first act of obedience was to tear down that altar and build a new one for the Lord (Judges 6:25–26). With that singular act, Gideon proclaimed, *"This chain of idolatry ends here."*

Timothy

In contrast, Timothy exemplifies what a holy inheritance looks like. Paul spoke of the sincere faith that first resided in Timothy's grandmother Lois and mother Eunice, and now flourishes in him (2 Timothy 1:5). Not all legacies are destructive; some are holy. Just as brokenness can be passed down, so can blessings.

These stories remind us that while family history influences us, it does not confine us. By God's grace, chains can be broken, and new legacies can emerge.

HOW CHAINS MANIFEST TODAY

Generational chains are not relics of the past; they are very much alive in our contemporary world. They manifest in various forms—some obvious and loud, others subtle and hidden—affecting attitudes, choices, and the ways we relate to God and one another.

WORDS

Words hold immense power. Proverbs 18:21 reminds us that *"the tongue has the power of life and death."* When a father repeatedly tells his son, *"You're worthless,"* that wound penetrates deeper than any physical injury. Over time, those words shape the boy's identity, influencing how he perceives himself, approaches relationships, and envisions his future.

Years later, without healing, that boy may become a father who, almost unconsciously, echoes the same words to his own son. The haunting refrain of "worthless" continues down the family line.

This illustrates the power of words: blessings build legacies, while curses perpetuate chains. Unless someone chooses to speak differently, the cycle continues.

ADDICTION

Addiction often flows through families like an underground river—sometimes concealed, sometimes evident, but always destructive. A grandfather who drinks heavily may dismiss it as "just the way men unwind." A father normalizes substance use as part of daily life. Consequently, a son raised in that environment may turn to the same substances when faced with stress or emptiness.

What one generation may dismiss as "just a drink" can ensnare the next as a full-blown addiction. Patterns of alcoholism, drug abuse, and behavioral addictions—such as gambling or pornography—can become chains that bind entire families.

Research supports this: children of addicts are more susceptible to addiction, influenced by both genetics and their environment. Spiritually, we recognize that addiction is a form of bondage—a chain that only the liberating power of Christ can break.

ABUSE

One of the most painful manifestations of generational chains is through abuse. A mother who was mistreated as a child carries unhealed wounds into adulthood. Despite her disdain for her past, these unresolved scars often shape her parenting. Harshness becomes the norm, anger becomes her primary language, and affection feels foreign.

Without intervention, she may raise children who carry the same wounds, passing them down to the next generation. Abuse may transform into new forms, yet it remains a chain. Even when outward behaviors change, internal scars—such as mistrust, fear, and lack of nurture—often resonate for generations.

But there is hope: cycles of abuse can be broken. When God heals the abused, they often become some of the most compassionate nurturers—those who, having experienced pain, intentionally pour out love to others.

FEAR AND ANXIETY

Generational chains aren't always overtly violent. Sometimes, they manifest in subtle yet crippling worldviews. Families marked by poverty, displacement, or trauma often pass down a legacy of fear. Parents who have endured scarcity may unintentionally instill a constant sense of lack in their children: *"There's never enough. Don't trust people. Don't take risks."*

As a result, children grow up enveloped in an atmosphere of anxiety they cannot articulate. They inherit worry as a standard way of life. Even during stable periods, they feel unsafe, perpetually waiting for disaster.

This is how fear perpetuates itself: not always through spoken words, but through the environment. A child raised in fear often absorbs it like oxygen—and later exhales it into their own home.

WHAT RESEARCH SHOWS

Modern studies confirm what Scripture has long revealed: unhealed trauma does not stop with one person. Research on *Adverse Childhood Experiences*

(ACEs) indicates that children raised in environments of abuse, neglect, addiction, or dysfunction often face increased risks of depression, chronic illness, relational difficulties, and more. Trauma creates ripples, impacting not only those who directly experience it but also their children and grandchildren.

While science provides us with understanding, Scripture offers us hope. Chains may be real, but they are not final. They form the backdrop against which God's redemption shines the brightest. When the cycle feels inescapable, Christ delivers a better message: *"Whom the Son sets free is free indeed"* (John 8:36).

GOD'S POWER TO BREAK CHAINS

The cross of Jesus Christ is mightier than any family curse. His blood speaks louder than the failures of your ancestors. When He proclaimed, *"It is finished,"* He declared the end of cycles that once felt unbreakable.

Galatians 3:13 states: *"Christ redeemed us from the curse of the law by becoming a curse for us."* The curse has been broken, allowing blessings to flow. In Christ, the inheritance of sin is replaced by the inheritance of grace.

Breaking generational chains requires both spiritual and practical choices:

- **Repentance**: Acknowledging the sins that have marked your family line and turning away from them in prayer.

- **Forgiveness**: Letting go of those who have hurt you, refusing to allow bitterness to define your story.

- **Renewal**: Replacing lies with truth, allowing Scripture to reshape your identity and behaviors.

- **Replacement**: Actively creating new patterns of love, blessing, and faith to pass on to your children.

You cannot change the family you came from, but you can change the legacy you leave.

I once spoke with a man whose grandfather was abusive, whose father was violent, and who found himself repeating the same patterns of anger in his own marriage. He despised himself for it, yet felt powerless to change.

One night, after a bitter argument, he broke down in prayer and cried out to God, *"I don't want to become what they were."* In the stillness, he sensed God whispering, *"It ends with you."*

That moment marked a turning point for him. He sought counseling, confided in trusted friends about his struggles, and began learning healthy ways to handle conflict. It wasn't easy, but step by step, the chains of his past began to loosen. Today, he is raising his children with gentleness and grace, determined that the violence of his past will not define their future.

His story demonstrates that generational chains can be broken. In Christ, transformation is possible.

REFLECTION SUMMARY

- Generational chains are real—cycles of sin, trauma, and brokenness passed down through families.

- Scripture reveals both destructive patterns and legacies of blessing.

- Christ's sacrifice on the cross is more powerful than any curse or cycle.

- Through repentance, forgiveness, renewal, and replacement, old chains are shattered.

- Your life can be the turning point where bondage ends and blessing begins.

Prayer for Breaking Chains

Father, I bring before You the patterns of pain and sin that have marked my family line. I confess the ways these chains have burdened me, but I thank You that in Christ, they can be broken. By the blood of Jesus, I renounce every generational curse and every cycle of addiction, abuse, or rejection. I receive a new identity as Your child, free and redeemed. Let my life be the place where old chains fall and new blessings begin. May the generations after me inherit faith, hope, and love. In Jesus' name, Amen.

CHAPTER SIX

THE HEALING POWER OF FORGIVENESS

Few words in the human vocabulary carry as much weight or provoke as much resistance as *forgiveness*. To forgive is to release, to let go, to liberate ourselves from the prison of resentment. Yet for many, forgiveness feels unattainable. The wounds are too deep, the betrayals too personal, the losses too devastating. We fear that forgiving means excusing the wrongs or pretending they never mattered.

Here lies the paradox of forgiveness: it is less about the offender and more about the one who has been hurt. Unforgiveness chains us to the past, while forgiveness unlocks the door to healing. To forgive is not to say, *"It didn't hurt."* It is to declare, *"The hurt will not define me forever."*

Scripture emphasizes that forgiveness is central to the Christian life. Jesus taught us to pray, *"Forgive us our debts, as we also have forgiven our debtors"* (Matthew 6:12). When Peter asked, *"Lord, how many times shall I forgive my brother or sister who sins against me? Up to seven times?"* Jesus replied, *"I tell you, not seven times, but seventy-seven times"* (Matthew 18:21–22). Forgiveness is not optional; it is the path of those who have been forgiven much.

Yet, forgiveness is not merely an act of obedience — it is a form of liberation. It serves as the healing balm that transforms wounds of bitterness into scars of wisdom.

WHY FORGIVENESS FEELS SO HARD

Forgiveness often conflicts with our sense of justice. Deep down, every soul yearns for wrongs to be righted. When we are hurt, a voice within us cries out: *"They owe me."* This sense of injustice is not only emotional; it feels deeply moral. Something sacred has been violated, and we ache for restitution.

That debt can manifest in various ways: an unspoken apology, lost childhood years, broken trust, unrecanted words, stolen opportunities, or lost innocence. The deeper the wound, the heavier the debt feels. Because this debt seems impossible to repay, unforgiveness often becomes a permanent companion.

Unforgiveness whispers, *"If I let go, they win."* However, the truth is that when we hold onto unforgiveness, it is we who ultimately lose. Psychologists note that unforgiveness fuels stress, anger, depression, and even physical illness. Carrying resentment is akin to drinking poison and hoping the other person suffers.

Spiritually, unforgiveness poisons our relationship with God. Jesus warned that if we do not forgive others, our Father will not forgive us (Matthew 6:15). This is not because God is cruel, but because unforgiveness obstructs the flow of grace; a clenched fist cannot receive mercy.

While unforgiveness may seem like a protective shield, it ultimately becomes a prison.

THE BIBLICAL CALL TO FORGIVENESS

Forgiveness is not a contemporary concept; it is the essence of the gospel. From Genesis to Revelation, Scripture depicts a God who forgives and calls His people to do the same. Humanity rebelled against God, incurred a debt it could never repay, and stood guilty. But God, rich in mercy, did what we could not: He sent His Son to bear our debt and restore our relationship with Him.

At the cross, Jesus uttered words that resonate through history: *"Father, forgive them, for they do not know what they are doing"* (Luke 23:34). These were not mere poetic lines or abstract theories; He spoke them while soldiers mocked Him, as nails pierced His hands, bearing the world's sin. Forgiveness is not a mere sentiment; it is a blood-bought reality.

Paul encapsulates this truth in Ephesians 4:32: *"Be kind and compassionate to one another, forgiving each other, just as in Christ God forgave you."* The pattern is clear: we forgive not because others deserve it, but because we have been forgiven by God. Forgiveness flows vertically from God to us, then horizontally from us to others. When we forgive, we reflect the very character of God, embodying His heart in a world that knows vengeance but rarely understands grace.

The Bible is rich with examples of individuals who modeled this kind of forgiveness.

1. **Joseph**: Betrayed by his brothers, sold into slavery, falsely accused, and forgotten in prison, Joseph had every reason to seek revenge. Yet, when his brothers stood trembling before him in Egypt, Joseph wept and said: *"Do not be afraid… You intended to harm me, but God intended it for good"* (Genesis 50:19–20). His forgiveness not only healed a fractured family but also preserved the future of a nation.

2. **Stephen**: As stones fell upon him, Stephen echoed his Savior, saying, *"Lord, do not hold this sin against them"* (Acts 7:60). Among the witnesses to his death was Saul of Tarsus, who would later become Paul the Apostle. Stephen's act of forgiveness planted a seed that would grow into one of history's greatest missionary movements.

3. **The Prodigal's Father**: When the wayward son returned home after squandering his inheritance, shame clung to him like tattered rags. Yet, the father ran — not walked — to embrace him. With a robe, a ring, and sandals, he restored not only their relationship but also the son's dignity (Luke 15:20–24).

These stories remind us that forgiveness is not a sign of weakness but an expression of strength. It embodies the power of God working through human hearts. Forgiveness restores what was broken, heals what was wounded, and opens the door to redemption.

FORGIVENESS DOES NOT MEAN

Forgiveness is often misunderstood, leading many to resist it. To forgive does not mean we deny the wrong or erase the pain. It does not guarantee that reconciliation is possible. While forgiveness and reconciliation are connected, they are distinct.

- **Forgiveness is not excusing.** Wrong remains wrong. Forgiveness acknowledges sin for what it is but chooses not to let it dictate the future.

- **Forgiveness is not forgetting.** Some wounds may never fade from our memory. Healing involves acknowledging the truth rather than erasing it.

- **Forgiveness is not reconciliation.** Forgiveness is a personal decision; reconciliation requires both parties to be repentant and willing.

- **Forgiveness is not weakness.** It takes far more courage to forgive than to harbor bitterness. Forgiveness embodies strength in its purest form.

Forgiveness is the act of transferring the burden of justice into God's hands, trusting that He alone judges rightly. It is saying, *"This debt is too heavy for me. I give it to the One who carries the cross."*

THE HEALING POWER OF FORGIVENESS

When we forgive, something supernatural occurs: we are healed. Forgiveness does not erase the wound, but it removes the poison that festers within it. The scar may remain, a reminder of past pain, but it no longer aches with bitterness. Instead of infection, there is restoration. Instead of torment, there is peace.

Forgiveness is not merely a moral choice; it is a pathway to healing. Modern research confirms what Scripture has taught for centuries: forgiveness promotes overall health. Those who forgive often experience reduced stress levels, lower blood pressure, enhanced immune function, and even longer lives. Our bodies are not designed to bear the toxic weight of resentment. Prolonged anger becomes a poison in our bloodstream. Forgiveness releases this toxin, allowing the body to find rest.

Emotionally, forgiveness unclenches the fists of the soul. Resentment tightly grips us, replaying the offense repeatedly and binding us to the moment of pain. Forgiveness loosens this grip. It acknowledges that the offense occurred but refuses to let it define our lives. When we forgive, the constant replay is silenced, making room for joy, hope, and emotional freedom.

Spiritually, forgiveness clears the fog that can cloud our intimacy with God. Bitterness acts as a barrier between us and His presence, dulling our worship, distorting our prayers, and making His voice harder to hear. However, when we forgive, that barrier crumbles. The channel to the Father opens, allowing His peace to flow in like fresh water on parched ground. Jesus made it clear in Matthew 6:14–15 that forgiveness is not optional for His followers; withholding forgiveness poisons both our relationships and our own spirits.

Moreover, the healing power of forgiveness extends beyond health and peace; it transforms our narrative. It replaces wounds with a stage for grace. Our testimonies evolve from denial — *"I was never hurt"* — to redemption — *"I was hurt, but God healed me."* The wound may not disappear, but it is reframed as a point of divine intervention. What was once bitter soil becomes fertile ground for His beauty to flourish.

This is why forgiveness is not a sign of weakness but a source of strength. It takes courage to relinquish judgment to God. It is an act of faith to declare, *"The debt is too heavy for me to collect — I release it to the One who judges rightly."*

As Lewis Smedes profoundly stated, *"To forgive is to set a prisoner free and discover that the prisoner was you."* When we forgive, we unlock the door to our own cell and step into freedom. As we move forward, we realize that forgiveness does not diminish justice; it entrusts it to God. It does not erase the past; it redeems it. And it does not deny the pain; it asserts that pain will not have the final word.

I once met a woman deeply wounded by her father's absence. His neglect left her feeling unwanted and unworthy, and for years, bitterness took root, shaping her relationships and her perception of God.

One night, during prayer, she felt God whisper to her, *"Forgiving him will not change the past, but it will free your future."* With trembling faith, she chose to release her father into God's hands—not because he had asked for forgiveness or deserved it, but because she yearned for freedom.

Later, she shared, *"It was like chains fell from my heart. For the first time, I felt peace."* While forgiveness did not erase her pain, it opened the door to healing. Today, she inspires others with the message: *"Forgiveness doesn't change them. It changes you."*

Her story serves as a powerful reminder that forgiveness is not about forgetting; it is about finding freedom.

REFLECTION SUMMARY

- Forgiveness is one of the hardest yet most liberating choices we can make.

- It challenges our sense of justice but frees us from bitterness.

- Forgiveness is the heartbeat of the gospel—we forgive because we have been forgiven.

- The Bible is filled with examples of men and women who modeled forgiveness, demonstrating its power.

- Forgiveness does not excuse or minimize wrongdoing; it releases us from its grip.

- The healing power of forgiveness transforms wounds into testimonies of grace.

Prayer for the Strength to Forgive

Father, I confess the times I have held onto unforgiveness. The wounds run deep, and forgiveness feels unattainable. Yet, I am grateful that in Christ, I have received immense forgiveness. Lord, grant me the courage to release those who have wronged me. Heal my heart, eliminate the poison of bitterness, and let Your peace fill my soul. Teach me to forgive as You have forgiven me, so that my story may become a testament to Your grace. In Jesus' name, Amen.

CHAPTER SEVEN

THE JOURNEY OF INNER HEALING

Maria grew up in a home filled with silence and shadows. Her father left when she was young, and her mother, overwhelmed by the burden of providing, rarely expressed affection. As a child, Maria learned to mask her pain through achievement. Good grades made her feel noticed, and success made her feel loved.

Yet, deep within, Maria carried a silent wound: *"I am not enough. I am not wanted."* This wound followed her into adulthood. In her marriage, she feared abandonment. At work, she constantly pushed herself, terrified of failure. Even in her relationship with God, she questioned whether He truly loved her or merely tolerated her for what she could do.

One night at a women's retreat, during a time of prayer, Maria broke down. Through tears, she confessed to God the truth she had hidden for decades: *"I don't feel wanted. I feel invisible."* In that stillness, she felt His presence envelop her like a warm embrace. She sensed Him whisper, *"You are My beloved daughter. I have always wanted you."*

That moment did not erase all her struggles, but it marked the beginning of her healing journey. Slowly, layer by layer, Maria allowed God to touch the wounds she had buried. Over time, the lie of rejection lost its power, replaced by the truth of God's love. Today, Maria shares her story with others, reminding them that healing is not about pretending the wound never existed, but about allowing God to transform it into a testimony.

Her story invites us to recognize that inner healing is possible.

WHY INNER HEALING MATTERS

Wounds that are ignored do not disappear; they deepen. What we bury alive stays alive. Unhealed pain does not vanish with time; instead, it festers beneath the surface and eventually seeps into every aspect of our lives.

Some individuals carry these unhealed wounds into relationships, where they manifest as mistrust, jealousy, or controlling behavior. Others internalize them, leading to chronic illness, fatigue, or tension in their bodies. Still, others struggle spiritually, finding it difficult to believe in God's promises or to feel His love because their hearts are burdened by unresolved hurt.

This is why Proverbs 4:23 advises, *"Above all else, guard your heart, for everything you do flows from it."* The heart is the wellspring of life; if the well is poisoned, the water will be too. When our hearts remain unhealed, everything that flows from them—our words, relationships, decisions, and faith—becomes tainted.

Inner healing is essential because our outer lives cannot thrive if our inner lives are broken. God desires not only to save our souls but also to restore our hearts.

THE WOMAN AT THE WELL

Few stories in Scripture illustrate the power of inner healing as poignantly as the encounter between Jesus and the Samaritan woman at the well (John 4).

She approached the well at noon (the hottest part of the day), when others chose to stay indoors. This detail is significant. Most women came early in the morning or late in the evening to avoid the scorching sun. However, she came at a time when she was least likely to encounter anyone. Shame had rendered her a social outcast. She had endured multiple failed relationships—five husbands—and was currently living with a man who was not her husband. Each broken covenant left another crack in her heart, whispering, *"You are not worthy. You are not wanted. You are too damaged to belong."*

Her story illustrates how unhealed wounds often isolate us. Rejection convinces us that hiding is safer than being seen. Shame leads us to believe that silence is preferable to honesty. Pain drives us to the well at noon, hoping no one will notice the ache we carry.

But Jesus noticed her. Not only did He notice, but He intentionally approached her. John 4:4 states, "Now He had to go through Samaria." Culturally, Jews typically avoided Samaria, opting for longer routes around it. However, Jesus "had to" go — not due to geography but because of destiny. He had an appointment with a broken woman who believed she was beyond hope.

When He spoke to her, He acknowledged her wounds. He gently revealed them: *"You have had five husbands, and the man you now have is not your husband"* (John 4:18). He named her pain, not to shame her, but to heal her. He revealed the truth and then offered her something greater: *"Whoever drinks the water I give them will never thirst"* (John 4:14).

This moment transcended conversation and was a form of inner healing. She had spent her life drawing water from wells that never satisfied — relationships, approval, belonging. Now, she discovered living water that could quench the thirst of her soul.

Her transformation was immediate. The woman who once hid from the crowd ran back into the village, exclaiming, *"Come, see a man who told me everything I ever did. Could this be the Messiah?"* (John 4:29). The same shame that had silenced her became the testimony that brought her community to Jesus.

This illustrates the power of inner healing: when Jesus touches the hidden places of our hearts, shame is shattered, lies are silenced, and our wounds become testimonies. The woman at the well reminds us that no wound is too deep, no past too shameful, and no heart too broken for the healing power of Christ.

THE PROCESS OF INNER HEALING

Inner healing is rarely instantaneous. It is a journey, often akin to peeling an onion — one layer at a time, tears included. It requires courage to confront what has been buried, patience to wait on God's timing, and faith to believe that His love is strong enough to meet us in our hidden places.

1. **Acknowledging the Wound**: Healing begins with honesty. Many of us cope by minimizing our pain: *"It wasn't that bad. I've moved on."* But denial is not healing. The woman at the well initially tried to avoid her community and evade Jesus' questions. Yet it was only when she confronted the truth of her past that she could begin to receive healing.

2. **Inviting God In**: Many of us guard our wounds tightly, hesitant to allow even God to touch them. However, Jesus approaches the core of our needs. He enters the everyday routines of our lives and seeks access to our hidden places. Healing begins with the willingness to open the door.

3. **Receiving His Truth**: Wounds often carry false narratives. Her broken relationships echoed the lies: *"You are worthless. You are unlovable."* Jesus countered with His truth: *"If you knew the gift of God... you would have asked Him, and He would have given you living water"* (John 4:10). Healing occurs when His truth dismantles the lies that our wounds have told us.

4. **Walking It Out**: Her healing was not merely internal; it transformed her actions. Once someone who avoided others, she now ran to the very village that had scorned her, boldly sharing her testimony. True healing always leads to new behaviors, newfound freedom, and greater courage.

My friend shared a testimony about a brother named James. James grew up in an environment of constant criticism, where nothing he did was ever good enough for his father. As an adult, that same critical voice haunted him, pushing him toward perfectionism and enveloping him in shame whenever he fell short.

Through Christian counseling and prayer, James began to recognize the lie: *"You are only loved if you perform."* Gradually, God replaced this lie with the truth: *"You are My beloved son; in you I am well pleased" (Luke 3:22).* The same words spoken over Jesus became a healing balm for James's heart.

Today, James lives with greater freedom, less driven by the fear of failure and more rooted in God's love. His story illustrates that inner healing is not about erasing the past but allowing God to redefine its meaning.

REFLECTION SUMMARY

- Inner healing addresses the invisible wounds of the heart and soul.

- Unhealed pain never remains hidden; it shapes our bodies, relationships, and faith.

- The woman at the well exemplifies how Jesus heals shame, restores dignity, and transforms testimony.

- The inner healing process involves honesty, invitation, truth, and ongoing renewal.

- God transforms wounds into testimonies and scars into stories of grace.

Prayer for Inner Healing

Lord, I come to You with the wounds in my heart that I have concealed. I bring forth the pain I've hidden, the lies I've believed, and the fears I've carried. I choose to open the door and invite You into these hidden places. Please speak Your truth where lies have taken hold and bring Your comfort where shame has settled. Heal me layer by layer, until my scars reflect the beauty of Your grace. I trust You to restore my wholeness. In Jesus' name, Amen.

CHAPTER EIGHT

RESTORING RELATIONSHIPS

David and his father hadn't spoken in years. Their last conversation ended with words so sharp that they cut deeper than either realized at the time. His father accused him of being ungrateful, and David retorted that he wanted nothing to do with him. Pride built a wall between them, and silence continued to add bricks.

On the surface, David moved on. He built a career, raised a family, and convinced himself that he didn't care. But every Father's Day, every birthday, and every significant milestone brought back the ache of unresolved conflict, like a splinter lodged deep in his soul. He could ignore it for a time, but the pain always returned.

One Sunday morning, while sitting in church, he heard a sermon on forgiveness. The pastor spoke a truth that pierced his heart: *"Sometimes the bravest thing you can do is take the first step, even if the other person never takes the second."* David wrestled with those words throughout the afternoon. Finally, he sat down and wrote a letter to his father. It wasn't accusatory, nor was it a list of grievances. It was simply honest: *"Dad, I miss you. I don't want silence to be the end of our story."*

Weeks later, his phone rang. It was his father. The conversation began awkwardly—shallow, cautious, and uncomfortable. But eventually, cracks appeared in the wall. His father whispered through tears, *"I'm sorry, son. I thought you hated me."* David found himself crying too, realizing how many years had been lost to pride.

Their relationship wasn't instantly perfect, but healing began that day. Slowly, trust returned. Over time, they rebuilt laughter, shared stories, and even prayed together. David learned an important truth: restoring a broken relationship isn't about erasing the past, but about opening the door to a new future.

WHY RESTORED RELATIONSHIPS MATTER

We were created for relationship—both with God and with one another. Loneliness was never part of God's design. From the beginning, He declared, *"It is not good for man to be alone"* (Genesis 2:18). The Garden of Eden exemplifies a perfect relationship—Adam and Eve walking with God and with each other in harmony. But sin shattered that harmony, introducing shame, blame, and division.

From that moment on, broken relationships became a central theme in humanity's story: Adam and Eve hiding from God, Cain rising up against Abel, and Joseph being betrayed by his brothers. Brokenness is a fundamental aspect of the human condition.

Yet, reconciliation lies at the heart of the gospel. God refused to allow distance to remain between Him and His children. Through Christ, He dismantled the barrier of sin and welcomed us back into fellowship. As stated in 2 Corinthians 5:18, *"All this is from God, who reconciled us to Himself through Christ and gave us the ministry of reconciliation."*

This means that restored relationships are not optional for the Christian life; they are evidence of the gospel in action. When we choose reconciliation, we reflect the heart of the Father. While broken relationships can be burdensome, healed ones bring freedom, joy, and testimony.

Scripture provides vivid examples of reconciliation that resonate with our struggles today. Two of the most powerful stories are those of **Jacob and Esau** and **Joseph and his brothers**.

JACOB AND ESAU

The story of Jacob and Esau is one of betrayal, distance, and unexpected grace. Driven by ambition and deceit, Jacob tricked his brother twice—first out of his birthright and then out of their father's blessing. Consumed by anger, Esau vowed to kill him, forcing Jacob to flee for decades.

As time passed, guilt weighed heavily on Jacob. When preparing to return home, he feared his brother's wrath. He sent gifts ahead to soften Esau's anger, but nothing could guarantee his safety. The night before their meeting, Jacob wrestled with God, desperate for a blessing before confronting his past.

When the brothers finally met, Jacob bowed low in humility, but Esau did the unexpected: he ran to Jacob, embraced him, and wept (Genesis 33:4). Years of bitterness melted away in a single act of mercy.

Their story teaches us that reconciliation requires both humility and courage—and that God can soften even the hardest hearts. Jacob's fear transformed into relief, and Esau's anger gave way to compassion. What seemed destined for revenge became a story of grace.

JOSEPH AND HIS BROTHERS

Joseph's narrative is one of betrayal transformed into redemption. Hated by his brothers for his dreams and their father's favoritism, he was sold into slavery, stripped of family, and left for dead. Betrayal can hardly go deeper than siblings conspiring against their own flesh and blood.

Years later, famine compelled those same brothers to journey to Egypt, where they unknowingly bowed before Joseph, now the governor of the land. Joseph had every opportunity for revenge, yet he chose forgiveness. With tears in his eyes, he said: *"Do not be afraid. You intended to harm me, but God intended it for good, to accomplish what is now being done, the saving of many lives"* (Genesis 50:19–20).

Joseph's forgiveness not only restored his family but also safeguarded the future of Israel. His story reminds us that reconciliation often requires us to see God's larger purpose. Betrayal is real, but so is God's power to transform it into a blessing.

The narratives of Jacob and Esau, as well as Joseph and his brothers, illustrate that no relationship is beyond God's reach. Humility, mercy, and a willingness to acknowledge God's hand can turn estrangement into embrace and betrayal into blessing.

THE BARRIERS TO RESTORED RELATIONSHIPS

If reconciliation is so beautiful, why do many relationships remain fractured? Why do families stay divided, friendships end in silence, and marriages crumble under the weight of unresolved pain? The answer is straightforward yet sobering: barriers obstruct the way.

These barriers often feel like protective walls, but in reality, they confine us as much as they keep others out. Identifying them helps us recognize and overcome their influence.

PRIDE

Pride stands as one of the greatest obstacles to restoration. It tells us: *"They hurt me; they should come to me first."* It demands that the other person acknowledge their wrongs while excusing our own. Pride can even masquerade as self-respect, persuading us that reaching out first would make us appear weak.

However, pride does not offer protection; it imprisons us. It constructs walls too high for reconciliation to surmount. What we perceive as strength often conceals fear and insecurity. Pride whispers, *"If I admit fault, I'll lose control. If I make the first move, I'll look desperate."* In reality, pride merely prolongs healing.

Scripture warns us in Proverbs 16:18: *"Pride goes before destruction, a haughty spirit before a fall."* Pride does not preserve relationships; it shatters them. Healing begins when we humble ourselves, just as Jacob did before Esau, choosing humility over self-protection.

FEAR

Fear serves as a powerful barrier, whispering paralyzing questions: *"What if I reach out and they reject me? What if nothing changes? What if they hurt me again?"* It convinces us that avoidance is safer than vulnerability.

As a result, we choose silence over the risk of rejection and distance over the threat of pain. However, avoidance does not protect us; it merely prolongs our suffering. Each missed holiday gathering, every avoided phone call, and every unresolved memory adds another layer of grief.

Fear often masquerades as wisdom: *"I'm just being cautious."* In reality, it keeps us stuck. As 2 Timothy 1:7 reminds us, *"For God has not given us a spirit of fear, but of power, and of love, and of a sound mind."* The courage to take the first step toward reconciliation comes not from ourselves, but from God's Spirit within us.

BITTERNESS

Bitterness may be the most corrosive barrier of all. It starts with an offense, then takes root as we replay it repeatedly. The hurt evolves from a memory into an identity. We no longer say, *"I was hurt,"* but instead, *"I am hurt."*

Hebrews 12:15 warns us to ensure that no "root of bitterness" takes hold, as it defiles many. Bitterness affects not just one relationship; it seeps into every aspect of life, poisoning our outlook, our joy, and even our relationship with God. Bitter individuals often lash out at those who try to love them because love feels unbearable when pain has become familiar.

Bitterness may seem like a form of control: *"If I hold onto this grudge, I won't be hurt again."* In truth, it enslaves us, binding us to the very wound we long to escape. Only forgiveness can uproot bitterness, making way for healing.

UNREALISTIC EXPECTATIONS

Another barrier is the belief that reconciliation must be immediate and complete. We envision dramatic reunions filled with tears and apologies, followed by instant closeness. However, real reconciliation rarely unfolds that way.

Trust, once broken, takes time to rebuild. Like a fractured bone, it heals slowly, requiring care and patience. Expecting instant intimacy sets us up for disappointment and can lead us to give up too soon.

Unrealistic expectations can place undue pressure on others, pushing them to change more quickly than they are capable of. Genuine reconciliation creates space for a gradual rebuilding of trust, allowing new patterns to emerge and small steps of healing to accumulate over time.

When the prodigal son returned, his father welcomed him home immediately; however, the son's journey of growth extended beyond that initial embrace. Restoration is both an instantaneous event and an ongoing process.

OVERCOMING THE BARRIERS

Barriers such as pride, fear, bitterness, and unrealistic expectations are significant challenges, but they are not insurmountable. Scripture reassures us that through humility, courage, patience, and God's grace, these obstacles can be overcome.

Humility dismantles pride, faith dispels fear, forgiveness uproots bitterness, and patience mitigates unrealistic expectations. What seems impossible through human effort becomes achievable with the Spirit of God.

The protective walls we build can come down, and when they do, the beauty of restored relationships shines more brightly than the years of division ever did.

THE PATHWAY TO RESTORATION

Restoring relationships is challenging and demands courage, humility, and perseverance. However, Scripture provides us with a pathway that is not a strict formula but a pattern of grace—steps that open the door for God to act where human strength falls short.

PRAYER FIRST

Every reconciliation begins with God. Before we pick up the phone, write a letter, or schedule a meeting, we must first kneel in prayer. Prayer softens our hearts, calms our defensiveness, and clarifies our motives.

At times, through prayer, God reveals areas where we need to repent. Other times, He helps us see the other person through His eyes—not as an adversary but as someone broken, like us, in need of grace.

Prayer also prepares the way for the other person. While we may be unable to change their heart, God can. He can cultivate compassion where anger once resided and tenderness where bitterness had taken root.

Jesus Himself exemplified this. Before going to the cross—the ultimate act of reconciliation between God and humanity—He prayed. He surrendered His will to the Father, finding strength to embark on a seemingly impossible path. Similarly, reconciliation in our lives requires a dependence on prayer.

TAKE THE FIRST STEP

Romans 12:18 states, *"If it is possible, as far as it depends on you, live at peace with everyone."* Pay attention to the phrase *"as far as it depends on you."* While we cannot control the outcome of relationships, we can control our own actions and obedience.

Taking the first step toward reconciliation may feel daunting. Pride may resist, and fear may sow doubts. However, healing often begins when one person decides to take that initial step. This could be making a phone call, sending a handwritten note, or simply asking, *"Can we talk?"*

Reconciliation does not require grand gestures; it starts with humble beginnings. Even if the other person does not respond, you can take comfort in knowing you have done your part before God. You have opened the door, and sometimes, that small step is all it takes to start dismantling years of silence.

Consider Jacob approaching Esau. He took the initiative by bowing seven times before his brother. That act of humility paved the way for Esau's embrace.

SPEAK TRUTH IN LOVE

Reconciliation demands honesty. Ignoring past hurts or sweeping pain under the rug does not heal wounds; it merely buries them alive. However, truth must always be accompanied by love. Truth without love can be harsh, while love without truth fails to address the real issues. Genuine healing requires both.

In Ephesians 4:15, Paul encourages us to *"speak the truth in love."* This means approaching difficult conversations with gentleness, humility, and a focus on restoration rather than revenge. We should avoid blame-filled phrases like *"you always"* or *"you never,"* and instead express our feelings: *"When this happened, I felt hurt. I want us to heal."*

Communicating love through our tone, body language, and intentions shows that our goal is not to win an argument, but to rebuild the relationship. Speaking the truth in love is about creating space for healing, not keeping score.

FORGIVE, EVEN IF THEY DON'T CHANGE

Forgiveness lies at the heart of reconciliation, yet it often must occur before full reconciliation can happen. Forgiveness releases the burden of the offense into God's hands. It does not mean we excuse the wrongdoing or pretend it didn't hurt; rather, it signifies our refusal to let bitterness control us.

Reconciliation may be partial, or in some cases, it may not be possible if the other person is unwilling to engage or if the relationship poses a risk. Nevertheless, forgiveness is always within our reach. You can choose to find peace in your heart, even if the other person never offers an apology.

Jesus exemplified forgiveness on the cross when He prayed, *"Father, forgive them, for they do not know what they are doing"* (Luke 23:34). Forgiveness does not rely on whether the offender changes; it depends on our willingness to entrust them to God.

Here lies the paradox: forgiveness liberates the forgiver even more than the forgiven.

REBUILD SLOWLY

Trust is delicate. Once broken, it cannot be mended overnight. Rebuilding trust is a gradual process—often two steps forward and one step back. It requires consistency, humility, and time.

Some relationships may never return to their previous state, but they can evolve into something new, characterized by honesty and grace. Restoration is not about instant perfection; it is about gradual growth.

Consider Joseph's story. He did not reveal his identity to his brothers immediately upon their arrival in Egypt. Instead, he tested their hearts, looking for signs of change. Only when he recognized their sincerity did he fully embrace them. True reconciliation demands wisdom—rebuilding at a pace that ensures both safety and sincerity.

Like a broken bone, trust heals slowly. If rushed, it may re-fracture. However, with patience, careful steps, and God's grace, what was broken can become stronger than before.

CLOSING THOUGHT ON THE PATHWAY

This pathway—prayer, initial steps, truth in love, forgiveness, and slow rebuilding—does not guarantee that every relationship will be fully restored. Some relationships may remain distant despite our best efforts. Yet, following this path ensures that we have done our part before God.

And sometimes, miracles do occur: the prodigal returns, the friend reaches out, the sibling embraces, the spouse forgives. Even when restoration is partial, peace fills your heart because you have entrusted the outcome to God.

REFLECTION SUMMARY

- We were created for relationships; brokenness was never God's design.

- Reconciliation is at the heart of the gospel—God restored us and entrusted us with the ministry of restoring others.

- Scripture demonstrates that reconciliation is possible even after betrayal and denial.

- Pride, fear, bitterness, and unrealistic expectations often obstruct our path.

- The pathway of prayer, humility, honesty, forgiveness, and patience opens the door to healing.

- Restored relationships reflect God's love and serve as testimonies of His grace.

Prayer for Restored Relationships

Father, You are the God of reconciliation. Thank You for restoring me to Yourself through Jesus. I present to You the broken relationships in my life. Heal what is fractured and soften the hearts hardened by pride, fear, or bitterness. Grant me the humility to take the first step, the wisdom to speak truth in love, and the patience to rebuild trust. Where reconciliation is possible, bring it to fruition. Where it is not, grant me the peace to forgive and let go. May my relationships reflect Your grace and serve as a testament to Your love. In Jesus' name, Amen.

CHAPTER NINE

WONDERS OF WHOLENESS

For years, Sarah felt as if her life was a puzzle with missing pieces. Her childhood had been marred by rejection, and her adulthood was filled with disappointment. She managed to function — going to work, raising her children, even attending church — but inside, she felt fractured.

She yearned for peace, yet it always seemed just out of reach. She often thought, *"Maybe if I fix my marriage, get a better job, or move to a new city, then I'll finally feel whole."* However, regardless of the changes she made in her external circumstances, the emptiness within remained.

One day, during a quiet prayer retreat, Sarah felt God whisper to her heart: *"Wholeness is not about rearranging your circumstances. It is about letting Me restore your soul."*

That moment changed everything. She stopped pursuing wholeness through achievements and began to find it through surrender. Over time, Sarah experienced not only healing but also joy. Her scars remained, but they no longer defined her. She started to notice beauty in the ordinary — laughter around the dinner table, the colors of the sunrise, and the grace of God in every breath.

Her story serves as a reminder: God does not merely mend broken pieces; He creates something entirely new. When He makes us whole, He awakens us to wonder.

Wholeness is not perfection. It does not mean living a life free from scars or struggles. It means living integrated — no longer fragmented by shame, fear, or hidden wounds.

The Hebrew word *shalom* beautifully encapsulates this. Often translated as "peace," it encompasses completeness, harmony, and well-being. When Jesus healed the broken, He frequently declared, *"Your faith has made you whole."* His touch was never about fixing one aspect of life; it was about restoring the person entirely: body, mind, and spirit.

Wholeness means being able to carry your story without shame, to look at your scars and see grace, and to be anchored in God's truth rather than tossed about by lies.

FROM WHOLENESS TO WONDER

But God does not stop at wholeness; He takes us further — into wonder.

Wonder is living with an awakened heart. It is recognizing the fingerprints of God in the everyday. It is waking up not with dread but with expectancy: *"Lord, what goodness will I discover today?"*

When we transition from brokenness to wholeness, the natural overflow is wonder. Our scars become stories, our pain transforms into purpose, and our wounds become windows through which God's glory shines.

The cross exemplifies this transformation. Once a symbol of death and despair, it became the very place where salvation was accomplished. What once represented shame now proclaims glory. That is the wonder of wholeness: God transforms what once destroyed us into a testimony that displays His power.

The Scriptures are filled with men and women who endured profound sorrow only to discover that God could turn their mourning into songs of wonder.

Consider **Hannah**. She longed for a child but faced years of barrenness. Her rival mocked her, her heart ached, and bitterness weighed heavily on her soul. Yet instead of turning away from God, she poured out her anguish before Him at the temple. With tears streaming down her face, she prayed for the impossible. And the God of wonders answered her. Hannah gave birth to Samuel, the prophet who would anoint kings and shape the destiny of Israel. Her story did not end in bitterness but in a powerful song of praise that still resonates in Scripture: *"My heart rejoices in the Lord; in the Lord my horn is lifted high"* (1 Samuel 2:1). What once seemed like a closed womb became the gateway to a testimony of wonder.

Then there is **Naomi**. Life dealt her blow after blow — famine, the loss of her husband, and the death of both sons. She returned to Bethlehem so burdened with grief that she told the women of the town, *"Don't call me Naomi; call me Mara, because the Almighty has made my life very bitter"* (Ruth 1:20). To Naomi, her story appeared over. She believed she had nothing left to give. Yet, in Ruth's loyalty, God was already weaving redemption. Through Ruth's marriage to Boaz and the birth of Obed — Naomi's grandson — joy returned. The women of the town exclaimed, *"Praise be to the Lord, who this day has not* *left you without a guardian-redeemer"* (Ruth 4:14). Naomi's emptiness was filled, her bitterness transformed into blessing, and her family line grafted into the very lineage of Christ.

Next, we see **the disciples**. After Jesus' crucifixion, they were devastated. Hiding behind locked doors, they were filled with fear and despair. The One they had followed, whom they believed to be the Messiah, had been nailed to a cross. Everything they had hoped for seemed lost. But on the third day, everything changed. The risen Jesus walked into their fear, showed them His scars, and spoke peace over their trembling hearts. Their despair gave way to awe, and their fear was swallowed up in wonder. These same men, once paralyzed by fear, became bold witnesses, transforming the world with the gospel. Their lives were forever marked not by defeat but by resurrection power.

Each of these stories reminds us: God does not merely heal wounds; He transforms them into wonders. He takes barrenness and births songs of praise. He turns bitterness into blessing. He transforms fear into bold testimony. The God of Hannah, Naomi, and the disciples is the same God who can take your story of brokenness and weave it into a narrative of wonder.

WHEN WOUNDS BECOME WONDERS

Wholeness is not just an idea to be studied; it is a reality to be lived. Around the world, countless men and women carry scars that once defined them — until God transformed those very scars into testimonies of His grace. Their stories remind us that wholeness is often supernatural, a work of the Holy Spirit that transcends human ability.

Joni Eareckson Tada — Wholeness Through Disability

At 17, Joni Eareckson Tada's life was shattered when a diving accident left her paralyzed from the shoulders down. Depression and despair nearly consumed her, but in the silence of suffering, she encountered the living Christ. Over time, God transformed her pain into a global ministry.

Today, through *Joni and Friends*, Joni has ministered to millions with disabilities, offering resources, retreats, and the gospel of hope. Her wheelchair did not end her story; it became her pulpit. As Joni herself has said: *"God permits what He hates to accomplish what He loves."*

Joel Sonnenberg — Wholeness Through Fire

At just 22 months old, Joel Sonnenberg was horrifically burned in a car accident that left 85% of his body scarred. More than 45 surgeries followed. For years, his reflection reminded him of loss. Yet God was writing another story.

Joel encountered Christ and discovered that scars can shine. Today, he is a motivational speaker and graduate, sharing with audiences around the world that God can turn tragedy into triumph. His wounds, once a source of shame, became his platform for proclaiming the gospel. His story affirms the truth: *your greatest wound can become your greatest witness.*

Bob Mortimer — Wholeness Through Loss

When Bob Mortimer was electrocuted in an accident, he lost both legs above the knee and his left arm. Addiction and despair had already plagued his life, and now tragedy threatened to destroy him. But in his lowest moment, Bob encountered Jesus Christ.

God transformed his brokenness into bold ministry. Bob became a traveling evangelist, speaking in schools, churches, and prisons. With his family, he hand-pedaled across the United States to share his testimony of hope. His life radiates this truth: *"God's strength is made perfect in weakness"* (2 Corinthians 12:9).

THE WONDER IN THEIR STORIES

What unites Joni, Joel, and Bob is not the nature of their wounds but the kind of God who met them in their suffering. Each discovered that wholeness is not found in erasing scars but in surrendering them to Christ. Each now lives in wonder — their brokenness turned into beauty, their weakness into strength, and their sorrow into ministry.

Their stories echo the promise of Isaiah 61:3: *"to bestow on them a crown of beauty instead of ashes, the oil of joy instead of mourning, and a garment of praise instead of a spirit of despair."*

The same God who did this for them can do it for you.

HOW TO WALK IN THE WONDERS OF WHOLENESS

Walking in wholeness and wonder is not a one-time event; it is a daily rhythm. It involves both intentional practices and the supernatural work of God's Spirit.

1. **Receive Your Identity**: Wholeness begins by embracing who God says you are. You are not the sum of your wounds or failures; you are a beloved child of God. *"The old has gone, the new is here"* (2 Corinthians 5:17).

2. **Renew Your Mind**: Trauma leaves lies etched into our thinking. Walking in wholeness requires replacing those lies with God's truth, day by day. Romans 12:2 calls us to be transformed by the renewing of our minds.

3. **Supernatural Healing by the Holy Spirit**: Wholeness is not only a process of personal growth — it is a work of the Spirit. The same Spirit who raised Christ from the dead dwells in us (Romans 8:11). He brings inner healing, breaks chains, and restores areas that human effort cannot reach. Sometimes this comes gradually through prayer and surrender; other times, it arrives suddenly in a moment of breakthrough when God's presence touches a wound too deep for words. Wholeness, at its core, is supernatural.

4. **Practice Gratitude**: Wonder flourishes in the soil of gratitude. Each day, acknowledging God's gifts — big or small — opens our eyes to His beauty and faithfulness. Gratitude shifts our focus from what's missing to celebrating what's present.

5. **Live in the Present**: Wholeness pulls us away from regret over the past and fear of the future. Wonder is discovered in the *now*. Jesus said, *"Do not worry about tomorrow"* (Matthew 6:34). The present moment is where His presence meets us.

6. **Serve Others with Your Story**: The scars God heals in you can become sources of healing for others. The Holy Spirit not only comforts us but equips us to comfort others (2 Corinthians 1:3–4). Wholeness multiplies when we pour out our restoration to help someone else rise.

REFLECTION SUMMARY

- Wholeness is not perfection; it is living integrated, healed, and anchored in God's love.

- Wonder is the overflow of wholeness — a heart awake to God's presence and beauty.

- Scripture shows us that when God restores, He always brings more than survival — He brings songs of praise, testimonies of grace, and lives filled with awe.

- We walk in the wonders of wholeness by receiving our identity, renewing our minds, practicing gratitude, living in the present, and serving others with our story.

Prayer for the Wonders of Wholeness

Lord, I thank You that You are not only the Healer of my wounds but also the Restorer of my wholeness. Thank You for taking my scars and turning them into testimonies, my pain and turning it into purpose. Teach me to walk each day in the fullness of who I am in You — complete, beloved, restored. Awaken my heart to live in wonder, to see Your beauty in the ordinary, and to carry Your presence wherever I go. May my life reflect Your glory and invite others into the wonders of wholeness. In Jesus' name, Amen.

CHAPTER TEN

MEETING THE GOD OF WONDERS

Every healing story has a turning point. Each wounded soul reaches a crossroad where they must decide: will I define my life by the pain of the past, or will I embrace the possibility of a different future?

For me, and for countless others, that turning point was not a therapy session (though therapy is valuable), nor was it simply the passage of time. While time may dull memories, it cannot truly heal trauma. The pivotal moment was an encounter with God — the God of wonders.

When people are wounded, they often withdraw. Shame whispers, *"Hide. No one can know. No one will understand."*

Trauma convinces us that we are unworthy of love, even unworthy of God. But the truth is this: God specializes in showing up in the very places we try to conceal.

Consider the story of the **woman with the issue of blood** (Mark 5:25–34). For twelve long years, she bled, deemed unclean by societal standards. Doctors had failed her. Her finances had run dry. Friends had abandoned her. By law, she was expected to remain hidden and isolated. Yet, when she heard that Jesus was passing by, something within her spirit declared, *"If I can just touch the hem of His garment, I will be healed."*

In that moment, it was not just her body that was healed — it was her identity. Jesus looked at her and called her *"Daughter."* For years, she had been labeled unclean, unwanted, and unworthy. In an instant, Jesus renamed her. That is what the God of wonders does: He meets us at our deepest wounds and bestows upon us a new name.

WHY ENCOUNTERS WITH GOD MATTER

Statistics and psychology reveal the devastating impact of trauma, but they also highlight something deeper: human beings need meaning. Dr. Viktor Frankl, a Holocaust survivor, once wrote that people can endure almost any "how" if they have a "why." Survivors of trauma do not heal by erasing the event; they heal when they discover meaning beyond it.

This is why an encounter with God is so transformative. In His presence, pain is not erased but reinterpreted. Shame does not disappear; instead, it is transformed into a powerful testimony. We come to understand that the wounds that nearly destroyed us become the very places where God reveals His wonder.

MY ENCOUNTER WITH THE GOD OF WONDERS

There came a time in my journey when I had carried the labels of rejection for far too long. I was weary of wearing shame like a garment, exhausted from believing I was unwanted.

In a moment of prayer, broken and vulnerable before God, I experienced His wonder. I heard Him whisper to my heart: *"You are not a mistake. You are not unwanted. You are my son, and I love you."*

Though it was not an audible voice, it resonated louder than anything I had ever heard. In that moment, everything shifted. I realized I did not have to live the rest of my life as a victim of rejection. I had a Father in heaven who loved me unconditionally.

That encounter changed everything. I still bear scars, but now those scars have become testaments to God's healing. I remembered the pain, but it no longer defined me.

BIBLICAL ENCOUNTERS OF WONDER

The Bible is filled with stories of wounded individuals encountering God and experiencing transformation.

- **Mephibosheth**: Crippled by a fall and living in Lo-Debar—a place of desolation and shame. One day, King David summoned him, not to punish but to restore. David offered him a seat at the king's table, declaring, *"You will always eat at my table."* From woundedness to wonder.

- **Rahab the prostitute**: Bound by a label and trapped in cycles of sin and shame. Yet, when she encountered God's people, she chose to align herself with His plan. Her act of faith spared her family and placed her in the lineage of Jesus. From woundedness to wonder.

- **Naomi**: Bitter and broken, returning from Moab empty-handed. But God restored her joy through Ruth and the birth of Obed, a child who would play a vital role in Israel's redemptive history. From Mara (bitter) back to Naomi (pleasant).

- **Zacchaeus**: a corrupt tax collector despised by his community. Driven by curiosity about Jesus, he climbed a tree to catch a glimpse of Him. Jesus paused, looked up, and said, *"Zacchaeus, come down. Tonight I must stay at your house."* This encounter transformed a thief into a generous giver, moving him from woundedness to wonder.

Each of these stories highlights a powerful truth: a single encounter with God can alter the course of a life.

WHY JESUS IS THE SOURCE OF RECOVERY

When you are wounded, your thoughts often dwell on your pain. You replay memories of abuse, betrayal, and loss, as trauma keeps those memories alive. Psychologists refer to this as hypervigilance — a state where the nervous system remains on high alert, constantly scanning for danger and reliving past threats.

However, the Word of God can disrupt this cycle. Romans 12:2 states, *"Be transformed by the renewing of your mind."* In Christ, your mind can be rewired, your thinking renewed, and your identity restored.

Jesus is the source of recovery because:

The Bible is filled with stories of wounded individuals who encountered God and experienced transformation.

- **Mephibosheth**: crippled by a fall and living in Lo-Debar — a place of barrenness and shame. One day, King David summoned him, not for punishment, but for restoration. David offered him a seat at the king's table, declaring, *"You will always eat at my table."* This marked a journey from woundedness to wonder.

- **Rahab the prostitute**: burdened by a label and trapped in cycles of sin and shame. Yet, when she encountered God's people, she chose to align herself with His plan. Her act of faith not only spared her family but also placed her in the lineage of Jesus. This was a movement from woundedness to wonder.

- **Zacchaeus**: a corrupt tax collector loathed by his community. Driven by curiosity, he climbed a tree to see Jesus. Jesus stopped, looked up, and said, *"Zacchaeus, come down. Tonight I must stay at your house."* This encounter transformed him from a thief into a generous giver, illustrating the journey from woundedness to wonder.

Each of these stories serves as a reminder: one encounter with God can change the trajectory of a life.

I have witnessed this truth firsthand in ministry.

- A woman who was abused as a child and lived in silence and shame for years encountered God during prayer and found the courage to forgive. She now counsels other women.

- A young man, burdened by alcohol addiction due to an absent father, responded to an altar call, surrendered his life to Christ, and is now leading worship.

A mother grieving the loss of her child found strength in God's presence, allowing her to continue living and honor her child's memory by helping others.

Each story is unique, but a common thread emerges: pain transformed into purpose when they encountered the God of wonders.

PRACTICAL WAYS TO ENCOUNTER THE GOD OF WONDERS

You may be wondering, *"How can I meet God in this way? How can I experience His wonder amidst my wounds?"*

Here are some steps:

1. Come Honestly

The first step is honesty. Healing begins when we stop pretending. God doesn't require polished prayers or rehearsed responses—He already knows the truth. What He desires is your raw heart.

The psalmists exemplified this approach. David cried out, *"How long, Lord? Will you forget me forever? How long will you hide your face from me?"* (Psalm 13:1). He didn't mask his emotions; he laid them bare before God. Jeremiah was so transparent in his suffering that he is often referred to as "the weeping prophet." Even Jesus cried out on the cross, *"My God, my God, why have you forsaken me?"* (Matthew 27:46).

When you present your pain to God as it truly is— broken, messy, unfiltered—you open the door for Him to meet you where you genuinely are, not where you pretend to be. Honesty is the gateway to encounter.

2. Seek Him in His Word

The Word of God is alive. Hebrews 4:12 states, *"For the word of God is alive and active. Sharper than any double-edged sword, it penetrates even to dividing soul and spirit."* Scripture does not merely inform; it transforms.

In times of pain, it's easy to let your suffering define you. However, reading Scripture daily allows God's voice to drown out your pain. It's not just a book—it's a love letter from your Father, filled with promises that reshape your identity.

- To the rejected heart, He says: *"I will never leave you nor forsake you"* (Hebrews 13:5).

- To the ashamed heart, He says: *"Though your sins are like scarlet, they shall be as white as snow"* (Isaiah 1:18).

- To the fearful heart, He says: *"Fear not, for I am with you; be not dismayed, for I am your God"* (Isaiah 41:10).

Each verse becomes a personal letter, whispering healing to your soul.

3. Create Space for His Presence

We live in a noisy world filled with buzzing phones, overflowing schedules, and constant responsibilities. Yet, God often meets us in the quiet.

Consider Elijah on Mount Horeb. Weary, depressed, and ready to give up, he found that God was not in the earthquake, the fire, or the wind — but in a gentle whisper (1 Kings 19:11–12). Elijah encountered God not in chaos, but in stillness.

Creating space for God might involve waking up a little earlier for prayer, taking moments of silence throughout your day, or dedicating time to worship where you allow His Spirit to minister to you. It's not about rituals; it's about being available. The more room you make for Him, the more clearly you will sense His presence.

4. Be Open to Community

God often reveals His love through others. Healing rarely occurs in isolation. As James 5:16 states, *"Confess your sins to each other and pray for each other so that you may be healed."*

A safe, Spirit-filled community offers accountability, encouragement, and tangible expressions of God's care. Sometimes, a hug from a trusted friend feels like the embrace of God. Other times, the counsel of a pastor provides divine wisdom. Similarly, the prayers of a small group can serve as God's voice, reminding you: *"You are not alone."*

Isolation reinforces shame, while community breaks it down by showing you that others have walked this path and emerged stronger — and so will you.

5. Expect His Voice

Many people miss God's voice because they anticipate it only in dramatic ways. However, God speaks through countless channels.

- Through His Word — verses that suddenly resonate with you.

- Through sermons — messages that seem tailored to your situation.

- Through the whisper of His Spirit — a nudge in your heart, a sense of peace, or a thought that aligns with Scripture.

- Through circumstances and people, God can use a conversation, a song, or even a moment in nature to communicate.

Jesus said, *"My sheep listen to my voice; I know them, and they follow me"* (John 10:27). You don't need to force it; simply expect it. Train your ear to recognize His tone, and you will find that He has been speaking all along.

WHEN TRAUMA REDEFINES, GOD RENAMES

Trauma tells us: *"You are broken."*

God reassures us: *"You are whole."*

Pain whispers: *"You are unworthy."*

God declares: *"You are chosen."*

Shame asserts: *"You are dirty."*

God proclaims: *"You are washed, clean, and pure."*

Encountering God does not mean ignoring our wounds; rather, it means recognizing that our wounds do not have the final say—God does.

REFLECTION SUMMARY

- Trauma often tries to define us through our wounds, but an encounter with God transforms our identity through His wonder.

- Biblical narratives illustrate how ordinary people found restoration in God's presence despite their wounded identities.

- Jesus is our ultimate source of healing, having borne our wounds and offering us new life.

- We encounter God through honesty, prayer, community, and Scripture.

- Though our wounds are real, the wonder of God is even greater.

Prayer for Encounter

Lord, I come to You with my wounds and the places I have hidden in shame and fear. Meet me here, God of wonders. Speak a new name over me. Where I have believed lies, replace them with Your truth. Where I have carried shame, envelop me in Your love. Heal my heart, renew my mind, and restore my soul. Let my story be defined not by trauma, but by testimony. In Jesus' name, Amen.

CONCLUSION

You have walked through a journey in these pages — from hidden scars to restored identity, from bitterness to beauty, from generational chains to freedom, from brokenness to wholeness. Each chapter has been an invitation: not just to read stories of others, but to see yourself in God's story of healing.

Perhaps as you read, you saw your own wounds reflected in Naomi's bitterness, Hannah's longing, Joseph's betrayal, or the disciples' despair. Perhaps you also caught glimpses of hope in their restoration. If there is one truth to carry with you from this book, it is this: **your wounds are not the end of your story. God is writing wonder into your life.**

Healing is not always instant. Sometimes it comes slowly, like dawn breaking through the darkness. Sometimes it arrives suddenly, like a flood of light. But in every case, it is God's work — a supernatural work of His Spirit, touching places human hands cannot reach. Wholeness is not something you strive to create; it is something you receive from the One who makes all things new.

And wonder? Wonder is the overflow. It is the joy of a heart set free, the awe of seeing God's fingerprints on your scars, the beauty of realizing your story can now give hope to others. Wonder is what happens when healing takes root and blossoms into testimony.

As you step forward, remember:

- **You are seen.** God never overlooked your pain. He has been present in every chapter of your life.

- **You are loved.** Nothing you've done, and nothing done to you, can diminish His love for you.

- **You are restored.** The cross declares that brokenness is not the final word. Resurrection is.

- **You are called.** Your healing is not only for you; it is also for those who will encounter God through your story.

So, walk boldly into the next chapter of your life. Let go of shame. Release bitterness. Embrace your scars as testimonies of grace. Live not as one merely surviving, but as one thriving in the wonders of wholeness.

And when you doubt, return to this truth: **Yes, you were wounded, but you are still a wonder.**

A Final Prayer

Father, thank You for walking with me through my wounded places. Thank You for the healing You have begun and the wonder You are still unfolding. I surrender my past, my pain, and my future into Your hands. Write beauty from my ashes. Turn my scars into testimonies. Let my life reflect Your love and invite others into Your healing. Help me live not as a prisoner of my wounds but as a witness of Your wonders. In Jesus' name, Amen.